I0835641

BEAUTY LOOKS AFTER HERSELF

The free man does what he likes in his working time
and in his spare time what is required of him.
The slave does what he is obliged to do in his working time
and what he likes to do only when he is not at work.

BEAUTY LOOKS AFTER HERSELF

Essays by ERIC GILL

Introduction by
CATHERINE PICKSTOCK

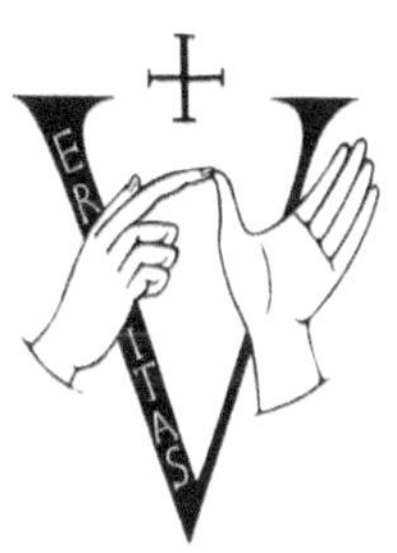

SOPHIA PERENNIS

Sophia Perennis reprint edition, 2012
This Sophia Perennis edition is a republication of the work originally published by Sheed & Ward, NY, 1933

For information, address:
Sophia Perennis, 36 Tom Holder Rd.
Ranchos de Taos, NM 87557
www.sophiaperennis.com

ISBN: 978-1-887593-44-1

Cover Design: Cristy Deming

CONTENTS

INTRODUCTION TO THE SOPHIA PERENNIS EDITION

> *"For it is easy to miss Him*
> *At the turn of a civilization"*†

PERHAPS we have all experienced the agony of uncertainty or indecision, a kind of poisonedness by the glut of possibilities. The feeling is not what one might expect—an excitement at the range of choices or a carnival celebration of opportunity—but rather one of wrenchedness, vertigo, sickness or stasis. The possibilities arraigned before the mind's eye, upon a flattened plane, become a kind of torment.

We are given a very different account of the phenomenon of choice by the mercantilists of our today. Is not material culture built upon the probity of maximum choice? Is not the display of manifold bright duplications inside our "glassy towers" a dazzling monument of gorgeous surfeit? Choice is now the measure of arrival upon the stage of the real: the more choices one has at one's disposal, the greater one's measure of power and command over the stage.

The range of the possible can sometimes beguile us. Its twinkly trinkedness can fool our animal simplicity, and we feebly follow in its trail of lights. But sometimes indecision in the face of the possible can account for a specifically

† David Jones, "A, a, a Domine Deus", *The Sleeping Lord* (London: Faber and Faber, 1974).

contemporary kind of dereliction, and this ought not to surprise us. For, as Eric Gill so straightforwardly understood, "Reality, what is real and not illusory, is what is sought by each and by all."

The problem with the possible is that it is not real, or not yet real, nor ever likely to be transposed into the real. And our romance with the possible, despite its attendant torment, is not something we can easily undo, for it is rooted in our contemporary philosophy and religion so deeply that it informs the very framework we peer through in order to discern its contemporary priority. And even before these historical changes, perhaps, it is rooted in our human and cosmic Fallenness. The dangerous lure of the possible lies in the fact that it can expand to any size and be of any colour; it can be lapidary or vaporous; it can be whatever we like; it is a rival infinity and can extend even beyond the limits of knowledge. Within the realm of the possible, we can aspire to be like God. So normative has the sway of the possible become that it is only in glimpses that one can catch a sense of its dominion and its corrosive simulated potency; or in moments of inspired protest, that we can gain a sense of how things might have been otherwise, or might yet be so—the anti-possibility of the end of the reign of possibility. Where, within the concealed and tarnished glories of the actual, might this be lurking?

In his essays, Gill refers, sometimes with unnerving swagger, to the great theoretical shift that took place between the God-fearing epoch of mediaeval Europe, East and West, and the relegation of customary, taken-for-granted Beauty from the Reformation onwards, accelerating beyond recognition during the machine age. For the first epoch, "beauty is incarnate love," and for the second, beauty and love are sundered, and beauty becomes "incarnate power." These two cosmic phases seem all-encompassing. Mundane, local disagreements between Capitalists and Communists, for example, are subordinated to a broader agreement as to the destruction of specificity and particularity. When beauty is separated out and fussed over as the rarefied, asphyxiating quarter of 'fine art', she quietly slips away from our daily grasp and her real all-infusing presence, so that all that is left is brute manufacture and alienation, on the one hand, and trivial adornment or decadent and ephemeral rarefaction, devoid of utility, on the other.

Eric Gill's broad-stroked and dualistic depiction of the phases of history might seem cavalier, and yet a glance at the serious metaphysical wagers underlying them are plain to see.

The main shift upon which his discourse on beauty pivots is the sundering of the so-called transcendentals of Being, Unity, Truth, Goodness and Beauty in the later middle ages. Until that date, from Plato to Aquinas, these had generally been taken to be convertible with each other, but this gradually ceased to be the case because of shifts in theoretical reason. The consequences were considerable. For, as Gill elaborates, if the presence of each transcendental is not implied by any of the others, then one cannot trust what is true also to be good, nor what is good to dwell in truth, or the integrally real; nor what is beautiful, or pleasing to the sight, to be in truth as it seems, and convertible with goodness.

These ontological, moral and aesthetic modes through which, as finite beings, the mainline theological tradition held that we apprehend the real, are themselves tied to a more fundamental framework, our relationship with God, which drives Gill's analyses of the phenomenon of industrialism and the state of contemporary art. It is no accident that when our perception of our relationship with God underwent a shift, our sense of reality and its relationship with itself, also altered. This change of framework was not a superficial or occasional perspectival reorientation, allowing one easily to resort once more to the earlier view if one pleased to do so. Rather, every level of perception was infused by the change, and this became self-perpetuating and soon the earlier view was eclipsed. The transformations in question began, as already noted, in the domain of theoretical reason but from the outset had immediate implications for the realm of practical reason, and were partly reinforced by somewhat self-evolving shifts: the rise of the power of finance capital, a non-reciprocalist market dedicated to the pursuit of profit, the rise of the policing and bureaucratic state trade, and a new sense of the autonomy of the individual human will.

In terms of our relationship to God, for Gill's favourite theologian, Thomas Aquinas, in keeping with the central Patristic tradition, the grammar of created being was articulated by a sharp ontological difference between God, who is being itself, and creatures, who exist in this or that limited specific fashion. Yet this cleavage paradoxically permitted a participation in the divine as the only source of being, and accordingly, an analogical resemblance to pertain between God and creatures.

But theoretical shifts before and after Aquinas, reaching a climax around the year 1300, in Duns Scotus' *Opus oxoniense*, asserted the metaphysical as well as semantic priority of Being over both the infinite God and finite being.[†] God was deemed 'to be' in the same univocal manner as creatures, although infinitely more so.[‡] This indifferent being, shared between finite and infinite, might at first glance seem to confer a degree of relation or proximity between the two units of reality: a more fundamental common transcendental, Being, now united human beings with God. But Scotist univocity introduced a separation between these two realities, because the infinity of the distance between them that was required in order to differentiate them, could be the object of no other concept than indeterminate existence, the most formal of essences, devoid of further determination save that of not

† John Duns Scotus, *Opera Omnia,* Lucas Wadding (ed) (Paris: Reedition of Vives, 1891–95). I have written in greater detail elsewhere about the theoretical shifts given expression in Duns Scotus' philosophy. See C. J. C. Pickstock, "Duns Scotus: his historical and contemporary significance", *Modern Theology* 21.4 (2005), 543–574; and "Modernity and Scholasticism: a critique of recent invocations of univocity", *Antonianum* [LXX–VIII] Fasc. 1 (Ianuarius–Martius 2003), 3–46.

‡ *Opus oxoniense* 1, dist. 3, q. 3; 1, dist. 3, q. 1; *Reportata Parisiensia* prol. q. 3, art. 1.

being nothing, and being of itself neutral, even as to truth and goodness, never mind beauty. One cannot peer intuitively through such an interminable quantity of sameness; this sameness Scotus declared to be beyond "every assignable proportion."†

A further component of the new way of articulating reality, which followed from the univocity of being, and which itself enabled the thinking of univocity, was the Scotistic 'formal distinction' of essence and existence. This is the term given to the kind of differentiation which is needed if one is to understand how indifferent, neutral Being relates to difference. For Scotus, Being, the object of metaphysics, cannot refer to the material being of singular units of reality because this would reduce metaphysics, supposed to be concerned with what is always transcendentally the case, to physics, which is concerned with the albeit general patterns of contingent motion and transformation. For this reason, there can be no material essence common to everything, since matter is the sphere of the inherently fluid and potential.‡ And yet the formal distinction of essence and existence is more than a logical distinction made only by the mind, and is ontological to the extent that each instantiated essence must occupy the neutral empty site of 'what is' in some distinctly apprehended fashion if it is to establish itself at all.§

† *Tractatus de primo principio* 4.78.

‡ *Opus oxoniense* I, dist. 2, q. 4, a. 5, n. 41–5, q. 7, n. 44; *Tractatus* 4.51.

§ *Opus oxoniense* III, dist. 6, q. 1; IV, dist. 11, q. 3, n. 46.

By contrast, for Aquinas' notion of the real distinction of being and essence, the particular nature of a thing participated in being. So, for example, water showed forth being itself in certain aspects of its unity, truth, beauty and goodness. But for Scotus' formal distinction of the two, all the properties of water, including its attractiveness and various uses, disclose nothing of being save the bare fact of its existence, which is the same old univocal existence that one discovers to obtain for earth or fire or air, or for that matter perfected steel or stage-paste. This barest being of being can be reduced to the logical negation of 'is not' just as the properties of water can be comprehended whether or not they are actually encountered in existence. And yet, in order for us to be able to say that a thing actually exists, given the assumptions of Scotus, we must say that existence has been conjoined with certain essential properties not just in logic, but also in reality. In this way, a semantic univocity migrates into an ontological univocity, since the being of water remains itself unrefracted by water, but is just jammed together with liquidity, non-opacity and so forth. Being and essence are here combined in a way that is less than fully real, because they are in no way inherently connected, even contingently, yet more than merely logically, because it is not simply that we are *thinking* the existence of water when we are bathing in the sea. But the same always-hovering virtual divisibility between the existence of water and water applies also for Scotus (as it did not for Aquinas) to the various different properties of water. Only by arbitrary divine *fiat* is water at once lovely, or else gliding and transparent, just as it is only by divine *fiat* that its existence is relatively unified, beautiful and useful.

So, being after Scotus is now both a bit real and a bit *not* real or 'irreal'. A being has begun to be a thing that is indifferent to existence and non-existence, as it is to actuality and potentiality. Ontology is on the road to becoming 'tinology' (the theory of things rather than beings).[†] It has also become, long before Kant, a science of the transcendental, because a minimally-determined logical existence (which simply 'is not not') is now seen as a condition of possibility for the actual reality of characterisable things.[‡] This new sort of transcendental hovers between the semantic and the ontological, instead of being, as for the older tradition, a more elevated universal feature of everything that is genuinely actual. This more airless transcendental being is also sufficient unto itself and no longer also unified, true, good and beautiful. These other transcendentals have been relegated to regional domains.

When being has become in this way a condition of ontological possibility, it reduces to being a mere condition of epistemological possibility. If the mark of actual existence is simply its logical determination as being 'not not', then we cannot be confident that being is anything more than something that appears to our understanding; we cannot be sure that it 'is' in itself. And the

† Jean-François Courtine, *Suarez et le système de la métaphysique* (Paris: P. U. F., 1990), 376–393.

‡ See Ludger Honnefelder, *La Métaphysique comme science transcendentale,* Isabelle Mandrella, et al. (tr) (Paris: P. U. F., 2002).

same thing will apply, as again for Kant (save for his attempt to elevate the ethical), to the now suburbanised transcendentals. Not only is beauty now relegated to a special department studied by the special new science of aesthetics which regards beauty as neither the desirable nor the useful; it is also only 'an effect for us'. Beauty is here depoliticised, sentimentalised, drastically subjectivised and removed from any disclosure of the real.

In the light of this account of the modern shifts in western mentality, it is easier to understand how Gill's insistence on the utility of art and its inherent link to the practical purposes of human life—both private and political—naturally went along with the idea that beauty is mystically disclosive of being.[†] While the formal distinction of essence and existence implies the new mode of transcendentality, the reverse also holds. For if being is less transcendental *ens*, than an assumed transcendental thingness nakedly necessary to all predication, then being is somewhat a being of reason, and yet also somewhat *not* a being of reason, in order not to reduce metaphysics to logic—that discipline for which there can be no concept whose definition is common to every being, since its concern is always to divide the self-identical from the purely different. One here acquires the space of a non-formal

† David Jones explored further the paradoxical coincidence of the '*utile*' with the wholly gratuitous, given that human culture, like nature, itself does not 'have to be'. See Rowan Williams, *Grace and Necessity: reflections on art and love* (London: Continuum, 2005), 43–94.

transcendental logic, as later articulated by Kant. At the same time, however, it must be somewhat merely semantic, because being as univocal is empty, neutral and abstract and therefore indifferent as to actuality and possibility. Because neither the real nor the intellectual distinction can exhaust this new object of metaphysics—univocal being—Scotus invokes, in effect, an intermediary formal distinction in order to situate what is neither a particular existing countable thing (difference) nor a universal, logically distinct intellectual being of reason.† This in-between is neither *a* being nor Aquinas' being *as such*, neither particular nor universal, just as it is neither real nor logical. It is captured in a "formality of being," as Eric Alliez describes it.‡

Scotist univocity is situated within the formal distinction, disclosing neither an empirical quality in common between things, nor any logical necessity for things 'to be' in a particular way. It seems in consequence to drain actuality from itself. Whilst Scotus deems univocal being to be actual, this actuality is instantaneously rationalised and vaporised in and through its transcendental univocity. So actuality becomes a kind of virtual reality, drained of the thrall of its particularity. In this way, one could argue that the west became subject to a new entailment of

† Honnefelder, *La métaphysique comme science transcedentale entre le Moyen Âge et les Temps Modernes.*

‡ Eric Alliez, *Capital Times: tales from the conquest of time,* Georges Van Den Abbeele (tr) (Minneapolis: University of Minnesota Press, 1996), 202–3.

self-bondage, endlessly lured by the glamour of the might-be and the imagistically-enhanced spectacle of the apparently real.

The same priority of essence over varying modalities of being which articulated for Duns Scotus the distinction between God and creatures, also shaped the difference between one thing and another thing, and (as we have seen in the example of water) between one thing and itself. So, in the case of God, he can possess formally distinct—rather than really identical and distinguished only from our perspective—attributes without (supposedly) losing His simplicity, which is grounded merely in the indeterminacy of Being, nor the *fiat* of divine will which now randomly decrees the unity of attributes in any finite reality.†

Likewise, the real unity of a creaturely whole is presented as the essential unity of nonetheless virtually distinct forms. This unity hovers halfway between logical and actual, for the substantive properties of a thing subsist in the same manner as the totality of the thing. At the level of ontology, they all equally 'are'. Although the lower constituents do not exist separately insofar as they are virtually contained within the given totality of the thing, a residual logical possibility pertains by which they could vie for priority over the whole.‡

For Aquinas, by contrast, the constituent parts of a substance (including accidents) only 'are' through the substantive form in which they inhere, so that the being

† *Tractatus* 4.51.

‡ *Opus Oxoniense* I, IV, dist. 11, q. 3, n. 47.

of a thing is continuous with its unbreakable unity, which forms the *telos* towards which it grows and in doing so manifests beauty. But for Scotus, real unity is undermined, while transcendental unity is methodically or formally undergirded: consideration of how things might be redistributed within neutral logical space now defines the unity they actually possess.[†]

Here, in consequence, the priority of the possible loosens the bond between essence and existence; the necessity of every realised essence becomes dislodged by the lurking chance of alternative natures. By formally distinguishing essence from existence, Scotus opens the possibility for a thing to be radically transposed into another thing, thereby relativising a thing in favour of all that it could be, rather than affirming the beauty of all that it actually is. Because of the potential independence of matter from form, and because of the evacuation of all analogical resemblances, being becomes unhinged from itself, destabilized by its own inherent yet extrinsic possibilities. Beauty can no longer look after herself.

Thus we have seen how the same double thesis of the univocity of being and the formal distinction has generated both the new virtual transcendentality of being, sundered from beauty as from goodness, and the new priority of the possible as the potency of the virtual that is supposedly prior to any lure of the actual. In appealing behind this modern metaphysics to Aquinas, the great

† Ibid., II, q. 1, n. 11; *Reportata Parisiensia*, L. 11, dist. 12, q. 6, n. 13.

consummator of classical and Christian tradition, in order to resurrect the modest prevalence of the beautiful, Gill therefore had it exactly right.

Eric Gill was confronting the results of modernity, at once in tune with and at an angle from the modernism with which he was contemporary. By comparison, the postmodernisms of our times may seem to have accentuated the trivial, the playful and the offhandedly ironic. Yet in reality the postmodern only accentuates what is implicit in the modern itself. For we have already seen how Scotist virtuality prepares the way for a modern priority of the epistemological, and so for a modern 'critical' metaphysics. It follows that the supposedly tranquil structures of post-Kantian metaphysics presuppose a radically unstable ontology of crossed-out actuality where things merely posture hoveringly over the void—as Friedrich Jacobi discerned in relation to Kant. Positions, whether ontological or territorial, had now to be held in place by sovereign will, by nervous contracts and treatises, by the assertion of decree or *fiat*, whether divine, princely or professorial.

For the traditional pre-modern view, by contrast, the actual had no prior hidden *mathesis*; there was no proper set of essentialised possibilities determining the modality of existence appropriate to any pre-given position. The in-between region where essence and existence, possibility and actuality, contingency and divine actual necessity combine, was not available to exhaustive analysis as to either a quasi-necessary or arbitrary arrangement. But from Duns Scotus onwards, this inexplicable in-between constellation is transposed into a pseudo-mysterious virtuality which embroiders its abstruseness from the constituents of self-division.

Actuality now testifies that its specific collision of characteristics is one of an endless arraignment of equally viable possible alternatives. These might never be actualized, yet they remain virtually present and qualify or haunt the necessity of realized possibilities. One might think of this as a kind of false or pseudo-plenitude, since every realized actuality must nervously look over its shoulder for a potentially endless series of competitors for its position in the real. The role of the actual thing in the encounter of cognition is here ousted, since the possible now demands formalization through a constant oblique insistence. The thinking of something becomes the criterion for existence and the ontological conditions of existing reduce to the transcendental conditions of comprehension. From here it is but a short step to a mode of knowledge which proceeds from a claimed *a priori* grasp of all fundamental structures of the real, combined with the nominalistic idea that for every distinct possibility there corresponds something countably distinct. The instance of the actual physical particular in our midst merely occasions our understanding. The thrall of its beauty is by the by; the lure of its truth is of no matter; its tarrying with goodness need not detain us.

At the time when Eric Gill first identified the shifts in philosophy and religion, the "turn of a civilisation" which gave rise to the sundering of beauty from truth and goodness, he could only have guessed at the way things would turn out. In order that we should not "condemn the unfamiliar," as David Jones put it,[†] Gill could still praise the motor car and other products of the mechanical age, as long as it was made well:

> [. . .] we are pleased by the sight of good machine-made things because we are able to recognise in them their admirable economy. [. . .] Their beauty is like that of bones and beetles and trees and flowers and the bodies of animals and human beings.[‡]

Such true utility is ineradicable from human craftsmanship even in a post-Lapsarian world.[§] Thus for Gill metaphysics took priority over history, even though history had abandoned the true metaphysics. For it must remain the case that the course of reality still obeys the contours of the true structure of being, even without knowing it. Hence while he might have railed against the brutalism of certain aspects of the machine age, beauty was still close at hand for him and could still be seen within modern life to take her place in the roundel of the transcendentals.

But as beauty has flown ever further from the fray of ordinariness to the enclave of finery, so utility, tricked out in all the trivial allurements of snobbish beauty's vulgarly pretty sisters, has been re-defined by an array of ever more

† David Jones, "A, a, a Domine Deus". See also David Jones, "Art and Sacrament", *Epoch and Artist* (London: Faber and Faber, 1959), 143–179.

‡ "Art and Industrialism", *Beauty Looks After Herself*, 198.

§ John Hughes, *The End of Work: theological critiques of capitalism* (Oxford: Blackwell, 2007), 198.

absurd inventions of new 'needs'. Utility has become a kind of decadent marketing opportunity. In the horizon of asymptotically receding possibilities, we are undone at each passing moment. For how, if we are hunched and nervously checking behind us, can we see what is really all around us?

For beauty is still all around us, circling and darting in and through her dance with truth and goodness. It is not these that have changed, but only us. The pillars and pylons, the concrete and the plate-glass are not in themselves at fault; it is only the positions we have allotted them, the way we have shaped and deployed them. And it is not possibility as such that has launched our downfall, for in the true potency of the actual lies the chance of the creative, the upbeat before action, the pathway of our imagination as the *conversio ad phantasmata* which restores the logos of the mind to its union with material particularity and the chance to project our visions outwards into the crafting of new realities. After all, Gill was not merely the celebrant of pervasively modest, if always beguiling, beauty, but also the proponent of "every man as artist," every man as the crafter of the liturgy of the ordinary.

Rather, our downfall is our enslavement to the possible as no longer regarded as rooted in given actuality and as reaching to a further participation in the infinite actuality of God. For this prior possibility of the virtual can only mean an already given *a prioristic* repertoire of what can be done, or else the sacred force of a nihilistic will to anything and nothing. In either case, the emergence of new beauty, which was Gill's overwhelming concern, whether in nature or in art, is absolutely precluded. For where the virtual rules, either there is nothing new under the sun, or else there is only what a cold fire enforces, an indifference which renders every new difference but the same sameness. This is a kind of Hell: when we do not realise we are already in Paradise, where even though beauty endlessly arrives and surrounds us, instead we seek to establish a fixed grid of categories and powers that cover over and seal-up the wellsprings of life itself.†

But even though she is all around us, with each passing moment, the sway of the possible grows ever more powerful. The glassy towers are built higher, the "dead forms" are projected more convincingly; the "inane patterns" and "trivial intersections" of univocity are increasingly mistaken for the real. The struggle to see the interwoven pattern of beauty, truth and goodness in the actual becomes ever harder to achieve.

It is eighty years since Eric Gill first sought to restore our vision, to encourage us to realign ourselves through festivity and craft with the dance of the transcendentals, and hurl ourselves back into the fray of the real. Now more than ever it is time to read him again, and see if civilization might not turn once more.

C. J. C. Pickstock

† Jorge Luis Borges, "Paracelsus and the Rose", Norman Thomas Di Giovanni (tr) *The Antioch Review*, 44.2 (Spring 1986), 133–136.

PREFACE

IT has been said that I am one of those writers who can only keep to the point by returning to it. I may say in self-defence that there are many readers who can only remember the point if it is repeated often enough. These essays, for all their differences of title, are really all about the same thing; they have only one point, and that point is very often repeated. I beg the perspicacious reader's forgiveness. At least I may claim that the connections are different; that though one phrase may appear in more than one essay, that is no more surprising or objectionable than finding the same free will in both the English and the Chinese.

What, then, is the point? I think it is stated in the last words of the last essay. I say the artist is simply the responsible workman; the art critics hail him as the irresponsible entertainer. I say he is a workman because his job is "the well making of what needs making"; they say he is an entertainer because Industrialism has released him from the necessity of making anything useful. I say he is responsible because, unlike a factory "hand," he uses his own powers of deliberation and choice; they say he is irresponsible because his works express nothing but his own fancies.

This art critic's view of art is widespread in our time. It is the necessary product of three centuries of commercial aggrandisement and the worship of money. In these essays, written upon a variety of occasions—a few because the spirit compelled me, most because I was invited to do so—I have tried to withstand the notion that there is an unbridgable chasm separating the artist from the workman, that the artist is a cultured person and a gentleman, and that the workman, having nothing to do with art, can only be cultured in his spare time. The pursuit of this theme can be carried on as well in a lecture on Prudence as in an address to a conference of British architects at Manchester.

A certain lady had a friend to share her box at a performance of *Tristan*. She talked all through the opera. At the end she invited him to come to *Parsifal* on the following night. He said: "I will come with pleasure; I have never heard you in *Parsifal*."

Here are certain opera: Prudence, the Church, Architecture, Sculpture, Industrialism, the People. If the reader can bear with me in one, he will be able to bear with me in the others. I only ask him to believe that, in spite of my dictatorial manner, I do not put these essays forward as final statements of truth, but simply as essays in aid of a grammar of practical æsthetics.

I am indebted to the proprietors of *The Golden Cockerel Press* for permission to reprint the first essay and to the Editors and Publishers of the *Journal of the Royal Institute of British Architects*, *The Architectural Review*, *Blackfriars* and *Architectural Design and Construction* for permission to reprint essays or lectures which originally appeared in their Journals. They have been revised and corrected for this edition, and are arranged in chronological order.

E. G.

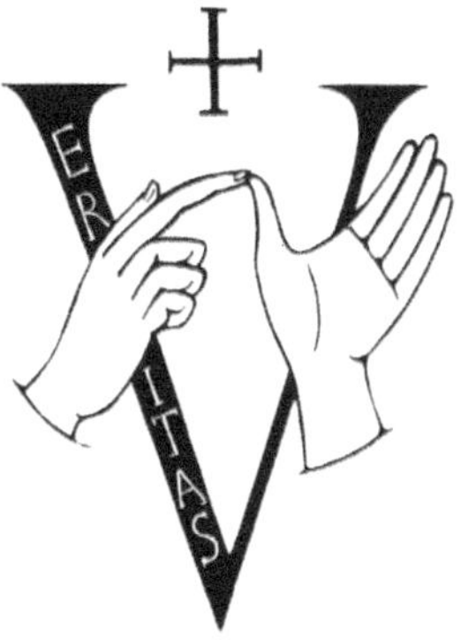
VERITAS

I

ART AND PRUDENCE

ART is skill—skill in doing or skill in making.
Whatever else art may be it is always that.

Skill is the body of art.

Deliberation is its soul or "form."[1]

Art is deliberate skill—skill with mind behind it.

"Art abides always on the side of the mind."

There is a thing called the mind of God.

Hence there is a thing called the art of God.

There is a thing called the mind of man.

Hence there is a thing called the art of man.

Only by metaphor do we speak of the art of the spider;

The spider, having no mind, cannot use deliberate skill.

The skill of the spider is directly dependent upon the mind of God.

The art of the spider is the art of God.

The art of the spider is like that of a factory "hand" —directed from outside. As the owner of

[1] Deliberation = The act of the mind in choosing. It does not necessarily require a process of ratiocination.

Form = The principle which determines a thing in its species.

I a jam factory said to a visitor: "I am God almighty in this place."

But man has a mind of his own and therefore free will.

A rational soul necessarily connotes free will.

Hence there is strictly speaking an art of man as well as an art of God.

But, unlike God, man cannot make out of nothing.

Man's mind, his intelligence and will, can only know the truth that God knows and desire the good that God wills.

Imbecility and ill will are privations.

¶ Skill in making and skill in doing are both loosely called art.

Doing is an activity directed to an end in view—the end in view being man's good, his last good, Heaven.

But when a man's deeds are directed not to his own good simply but to the good of a *thing*, then doing becomes *making*.

An act that is good, or thought to be good, with regard to oneself is called a *prudent* act.

An act that is good, or thought to be good, with regard to a thing to be made is called *art*.

A man whose acts are conformed to his own good is called a *prudent man*.

A man whose acts are conformed to the good of things is called an *artist*. I

In both cases skill in doing is required.

Skill in doing good to oneself is called *prudence.*

Skill in doing good to things is called *art.*

Prudence is the means to happiness in oneself.

Art is the means to pleasure in what is not oneself.

To have happiness is the object of prudence.

Happiness in oneself is a good and is the object of the will.

Happiness is subjective.

To have pleasure in things is the object of art.

Pleasure in things is a good and is the object of the intelligence.

Pleasure is objective.

Great intelligence is not necessary for prudence (happiness).

Great prudence is not necessary for intelligence (pleasure).

A fool may be a saint.

A villain may be an artist.

A fool may be a villain.

A saint may be an artist.

But a fool cannot be an artist, nor a villain a saint.

I ¶ Ethics is the science of happiness in oneself.
Æsthetics is the science of pleasure in things.
Both are departments of philosophy.
Prudence is the application of ethics to practice.
Art is the application of æsthetics to practice.
The practice of prudence is called morals.
The practice of art is called craft or craftsmanship.

¶ Happiness being man's goal, his final goal, it behoves a man to be a prudent man; for prudence has man's final happiness for its object.
But happiness is a state of mind.
It is that state of mind in which what is desired is known.
Final happiness is the state of mind in which the desired good is the known good—
In which the desired God is the known God.
When what is desired is known it is said to be *seen*.
Final happiness is to see God.
This is called "the Beatific Vision."
Happiness is, therefore, not a state of bliss merely;
It is a state of bliss in knowledge.
But knowledge is necessarily knowledge of something—not of *no* thing.
Happiness is in a knowledge of that thing or those things that are pleasing.

Happiness is in knowledge of those things that are pleasing to the mind. I

Those things are pleasing to the mind which are in themselves good.

God alone is good.

So those things are pleasing to the mind which are of God or in God.

Here below we may see God in all things (that is earthly happiness).

We may see through all things to God.

The state of Heaven is that in which we see all things in God.

We see through God to all things.

The prudent man acts so that he may achieve the blissful state of heavenly happiness.

But that state is one in which he has knowledge of all things in God—*Gaudium de veritate.*

Happiness is therefore not separable from pleasure in things.

Prudence is therefore not separable from art.

As making has need of doing—so prudence has need of art.

The achieving of happiness in oneself is the business of prudence.

The supplying of pleasure in things is the business of art.

I Art and prudence are, as it were, one flesh.

There is a marriage between them.

There is also a lovers' quarrel between them.

Each seeks the perfection of its own.

¶ Now man taken abstractly as the bride of God is female.

Hence the Church is the bride of Christ.

Man and the Church are one.

The clergy alone are not the Church.

The laity alone are not the Church.

Man united to God is the Church.

Man taken abstractly in his collaboration with God, i.e. as maker, is male.

Man the artist is male.

But, unlike God, he is not creator of things out of nothing.

He is creator in the second degree.

He is a channel, a vehicle for God's creative power.

Through man God brings creation to a greater and more poignant degree of beauty.

Art improves on Nature.

That is what it is for.

Beauty is the splendour of Being.

The beautiful thing is that which being seen pleases.

The beautiful is therefore the object of art, for only beautiful things give pleasure to the mind, and the pleasure of the mind is the object of art. I

The skill of the artist has for its end the production of things which shall give pleasure being seen.

Being seen means being desired and known.

But this pleasure is not the pleasure of knowing.

It is the pleasure of knowing the thing seen.

¶ The Church is man in his aim of achieving happiness.

She is therefore the guardian of faith and morals.

She is the mouthpiece of Prudence.

The Church is Prudent Man.

The Church is man knowing and acting in accordance with his end—happiness in Heaven—the Beatific Vision.

The artist is man in his aim of making what shall give pleasure.

Happiness feeds on pleasure.

Pleasant things are the meat and drink of happiness.

The ultimate happiness is heaven: for union with God is union with the source of all good

I and therefore with all things that are pleasing.

¶ Now the perfectly prudent man is a man of perfectly good will.

The perfect artist is a man of perfectly good sense.

Perfectly good will is, it seems, possible to man.

Perfectly good sense is, it seems, not possible to man.

His finite condition deprives him of the possibility of perfect knowledge.

Moreover, the perfection of good will is passive:—

"Grant that I may love thee always: then do with me what thou wilt," and again: "Be it done to me according to thy word."

But perfectly good sense is active.

(The words of God effect what they signify.)

Man can be perfectly passive.

Man cannot be perfectly active.

He can do nothing of himself.

"We are not able to please thee by our own acts."

Man can only be a perfectly willing agent.

His free will does not give him creative power.

It gives him simply perfect power to will what God wills.

A finite intelligence does not give him perfect knowledge of what God knows. I

Hence prudence is superior to art with regard to man, but "art . . . metaphysically is superior to prudence."[1]

¶ Man *taken abstractly* is both female and male.

He is both man of prudence and artist.

He is both churchman and statesman.

In the concrete, man is divided.

Church and State are separated.

Prudence and art are opposed—not as enemies but as lovers.

In the concrete, Church and prudence take precedence of government over State and art.

And each seeks the perfection of its own.

But in the modern world this right and proper opposition is obscured.

It is obscured by the tyranny of commerce—by the tyranny of the middleman, conveniently so called because he stands in the middle obstructing everything and obstructing particularly the marriage of art and prudence.

The servant has become the master.

The go-between has become the boss.

[1] Maritain, *Art and Scholasticism* (English translation, p. 84).

I In the welter the Church, in the order of doing, seeks to salvage what she can for prudence.

In the order of making, the State salvages what it can for art.

Under these circumstances the prudent man often becomes a prig and the artist often becomes merely a purveyor of sentimental trifles.

¶ Under a régime of commercial insubordination the mass of men are neither men of prudence nor artists.

But a semblance of prudence is more in evidence than even a semblance of art.

Worldly prudence makes a better show of virtue than worldly art.

To make money, to achieve material security and prosperity, looks more virtuous than to make what is merely pleasing.

Stock-broking morality and the morality of manufacturers and bankers stinks less in the nostrils of the prudent man, with his eye on Heaven, than does the art of music-halls or of dancing-places.

Such morality seems to be directed to the indubitably legitimate end of making money for the support of families.

There seems no doubt that men must live and must support their families. I

On the other hand, music-hall art and such like seems to be directed to no known end but worldly pleasure.

The prudent man looks askance at it.

¶ St. Augustine said: "Love God and do what you will."

Dilige Deum et fac quod vis.

The artist says: "Love and make what you like."

This is the highest prudence.

But the prudent man thinks them dangerous sayings: for though most men know what they like doing or making, few men know certainly that they love God.

Nevertheless, these rules are the only really safe rules.

It is the business of the prudent man to inculcate the love of God.

The love of God involves acceptance of what God has revealed and obedience to His law.

But "the service of God is perfect freedom."

This is not because love makes the law of no effect but because he who loves God loves what God loves.

"As the eyes of servants are upon the hands of their masters, as the eyes of a maid-

I servant are upon the hands of her mistress, so are our eyes upon the Lord our God."

So also the obedience of a wife to her husband spells neither sin nor servility.

But in the modern world prudence is rare—though seemingly less rare than art.

Our governors, the men of business, our rich men, are struggling for power.

Our workmen, we poor men, are struggling for worldly pleasure.

The Church is powerless.

Statesmen are at the mercy of financiers.

Saints and artists are but hot-house plants—eccentrics.

But though sanctity be peculiar, prudence has the lip-service of rich men.

Honesty still remains the best policy.

"Safety first" becomes the best catch-word.

Happiness is still desirable.

And though it be a hot-house plant, art also has the lip-service of rich men.

The appetite for pleasure still requires satisfaction.

But, in a world in which man's last end has been forgotten or denied, the pursuit of worldly happiness seems less dangerous than the pursuit of worldly pleasure. I

Therefore worldly happiness seems less an enemy than worldly pleasure.

The man who seeks happiness here below is looked upon more kindly than he who seeks pleasure.

The man of business is looked upon more kindly by the man of prudence than is the artist.

For the man of business ministers to happiness, though only worldly happiness.

But the artist ministers to pleasure, and often the pleasure of the senses merely.

Avarice seems less hideous to the prudent man than *Idolatry*.

Selfishness seems less damnable to him than *Sensuality*.

There is therefore some ill-feeling between the prudent man and the artist.

The lovers' quarrel between art and prudence has become an unloving "scrap."

The opposition has become a conflict.

The man of prudence is shocked by the artist's inclination to value things as ends in themselves—

Worth *making* for their own sakes—

I Loved for their beauty.
He sees *idolatry* at the end of that road.
He is also shocked by the artist's acceptance of all things of sense as beautiful and therefore pleasing in themselves—
Worth *having* for their own sakes—
Loved for their pleasantness.
He sees sensuality at the end of that road.
Upon the other hand, the artist is shocked by the prudent man's inclination to see things merely as means to ends—
Not worth anything for their own sakes—
Their beauty neither seen nor loved.
He sees Manchester at the end of that road.
He is also shocked by the prudent man's inclination to see in the pleasures of sense mere filthiness.
To him that is a kind of blasphemy.
The prudent man accuses the artist of sin.
The artist cries "blasphemer" in reply.
They see no good in one another.
¶ It is not for me to speak as a man of prudence—though the artist is a man and should be a prudent man.
I can only speak as artist.

As artists it is for us to see all things as ends in themselves— I

To see all things in God and God is the end—

To see all things as beautiful in themselves.

"The beauty of God," says St. Thomas Aquinas, quoting Denis, "is the cause of the being of all that is."[1]

It is for us to see things as worth making for their own sakes, and not merely as means to ends.

We are not "welfare workers."

We do not even seek "to leave the world better than we found it."

We are as children making toys for men and God to play with, and "playing before him at all times."[2]

But this serious view is not taken by many men of prudence.

Theirs is the frivolous view that things are not worth anything in themselves.

Clothes, for instance, are not for us as they seem to be for the prudent man, merely useful protections against cold or unchastity.

Clothes are primarily for dignity and adornment.

[1] St. Thomas Aquinas, *de Divinis Nominibus,* lect. 5.

[2] *Vulgate,* Proverbs viii. 30, 31.

I Whether men and women go naked, or whether they go clothed as monks and nuns, or whether they go half naked or half clothed like our mothers and sisters —it is all one to us.

It is for them to decide—and their pastors.

We merely ask that they be beautiful—that they be things which give pleasure being seen.

What else should anyone ask?

Trains, for instance: suppose two trains go from Manchester to London; one through a stinking and noisy tunnel all the way, the other silently through green valleys. Which train would a sensible person take?

Your prudent man, it seems, having regard merely to the end of the journey, would ask simply which was the quicker route.

Your artist, your practical man (for art is a virtue of the practical intelligence) would ask which would make the journey better in itself—as a journey.

¶ Let us return to the beginning.

Prudence is concerned with the man.

Art is concerned with the thing. I

Man is more important than things.

Prudence is more important than art.

Man's end is happiness.

The end of art is pleasure.

But happiness consists in pleasure.

Happiness is the state of being *pleased* with things, of being pleased with *things.*

Making pleasing things is the business of art.

The pleasure of the senses is good.

Art which aims at pleasing the mind through the senses is good.

The pleasure of the mind is good.

Art which aims at pleasing the mind and in regard to which the senses are disinterested is good.

But man is matter and spirit—

Both are real and both good.

An art which pleases the senses only and does not make its appeal to the whole man is necessarily bad art.

An art which makes its appeal to the mind only and does not please the whole man is necessarily bad art.

That is good art which pleases the senses as they ought to be pleased and the mind as it ought to be pleased.

I ¶ With good art prudence should have no quarrel;

God gave man senses that man should have pleasant feelings.

The reasonable pleasure of the senses is the God-designed reward of those acts, such as eating and "sleeping," which God wills men to do.

¶ With good art prudence should have no quarrel;

God gave men minds wherewith to have pleasant thoughts.

The reasonable pleasure of the mind is the reward of those acts which are called contemplative: that is to say: the vision of Being, the vision of things as ends.

But many prudent men quarrel with art, however good, because many prudent men are prudes.

The prude is afraid of the pleasure of the senses.

And many prudent men quarrel with art, however good, because many prudent men are proud.

The proud man scorns anything not in imitation of himself: that is to say: he scorns anything which has not himself for its end.

These quarrels can never be settled until most men 1
of prudence are also artists and most
artists have become men of prudence.

This pleasing state of affairs will not come about
until the present civilisation has passed
away.

II

REPOSITORY ART

REPOSITORY Art is the name given to the things sold in places called "Catholic Repositories." It is remarkable that things should get so bad without anybody being to blame. For nobody is to blame. It is nobody's fault. No one need go to confession and accuse himself of sin. The shopkeepers are virtuously trying to make as much money as they can in order to support their wives and families. The shop assistants are doing the same, and we may assume that, behind the scenes, manufacturers and their employees are not behind in their enthusiasm for the same highly moral end—the support and enrichment of their families. Yet the stuff is bad—the laughing-stock of all cultured outsiders, the weeping-stock of all cultured Catholics. Who would be cultured? But wait: does it matter whether we be cultured or not? In the opinion of the clergy, no, not a bit. "A man can be a very good Catholic in a factory," they say, and the saying cannot be too often repeated. To be a good Catholic—to keep the Ten Commandments and the commandments of the Church—is all that matters. They are obviously right from their point of view as pastors. Moreover, they are right from our point of view also. The

Catholic Church is not a cultured set. She will never II
be a cultured set—a set having a culture different from or better than that in which she moves. The fact of mediæval architecture, painting, sculpture, calligraphy—what not—need not mislead us: the culture of that time was a Catholic culture only in the sense that it was the culture of the time in which the great majority of men, women, and children were Catholics, in which the underlying ideas of justice, of trading, of society were Catholic ideas or ideas fostered by the Church or, at least, ideas to which she was not antagonistic. The culture of that time was not Catholic in the sense that it was in any way a direct product of the Church or of ecclesiastics. It was not any more then than it is now the business of the Church or of her ministers to dictate to builders or to any other kind of artist—except in the same way as any good customer is able to dictate to those whom he employs. It is no more than a superstition—the sort of superstition the sentimental and muddle-headed nineteenth century would naturally wallow in—that bishops and clergy were connoisseurs of art, and in many cases working artists themselves, and were able to impose their ideas, their culture, on a more or less uncultured working people. Even though it be true that many

monks and nuns were builders, painters, scribes, it is to be remembered that the religious life was not and is not necessarily an ecclesiastical life. Monks were, until comparatively recently, generally not priests; they were simply laymen bound by vows to a rule of religion. The Benedictines especially, that great civilising power, were, as may be seen from the rule of St. Benedict, not even expected to become priests and, still less, parish priests. In fact, the civilising power of man is a lay power—fostered, encouraged, nursed, petted by the Church, but, in its own sphere, independent. And in her sphere the Church is independent also. Man the artist is male —man the churchman is female; she takes what she is given.

Let us be studiously clear about this. In the sphere of faith and morals the Church is supreme and infallible. Hence her inestimable service to art; she makes the rails upon which we may run; she saves man from himself; she provides a regimen, a discipline without which man runs amok in his lusts and prides. All religions render this service—some better than others—Catholicism, obviously to us, need it be said? best of all. But the autonomy of the Church in faith and morals does not destroy; on the contrary, it supports the autonomy of man the artist

in the sphere of work and art and civilisation and II
culture. (Hence, incidentally, if we understand the controversy rightly, the official proscription of L'*Action française*—a newspaper and an organisation which on their theoretical side sought to make it out that Catholicism was bound to a particular politics, thus destroying the political and cultural and civilising autonomy of man. Again, the Church has saved man from himself.) But in times like the present, wherein man the artist has been submerged—so that the word artist now denotes a particular kind of hot-house plant, an eccentric, or a lap dog, and art either a merely decorative addition to otherwise ugly things or an activity directed to the making of quite isolated *jeux d'esprit*, a thing entirely unrelated to the life of the time—a time wherein the power of the Church herself has been submerged—so that the word religion means some sort of specially pious behaviour or opinion, and the word church may mean one or other of a thousand contradictory sects, and there is, even in a country like England, which has an *Established* Church, no sort of connection between the religious opinions of the people and their daily life—no sort of correspondence between their established religion and their culture—in a time like this it is inevitable that the issues should be con-

II fused, and as the artists, in their efforts to win back what commerce and commercial insubordination have destroyed, very often attempt to take what is not theirs, to make themselves self-sufficient in matters of faith and morals, as well as in workshop or political practice; so the churchman, the priest, the man of prudence, theologically so called, in his efforts to save souls from the wreckage, will very often seize what is not his, and will attempt to impose his authority in a sphere in which he has no mandate. As in France, as it appears, political Royalism is being put forward as the only Catholic politics, or as in England there is being made, in some quarters, an attempt to make out that a certain kind of simple, self-supporting, country life is the only life for good Christian people, so in the business of what is particularly called "art" we are expected to submit to the domination of the priest in the matter of ecclesiastical architecture and images.[1] In all these cases the man of prudence is infringing on the autonomy of the artist, or vice versa. The man of commerce, of course, knowing where his money is, lays himself out to flatter these tyrants

[1] Though it is a remarkable fact that the only period of Church history when ecclesiastics did really set out, on a grand scale, to be "art patrons" is the period (sixteenth century) wherein the art of public worship, the liturgy, was ruined.

—architects and other artists succumb to the ruling mania, and what the Catholic Repositories produce is only a cheaper and nastier variety of what our church architects love. To live according to the law of reason is what the Catholic Church above all things desires of us (the heresy of Luther is no more, at bottom, than a denial of this), but should we attempt to *work* according to the law of reason we get but scanty encouragement, and, for the most part, frank enmity and scorn.

Nevertheless, we are not here concerned to make complaint: we are neither surprised nor annoyed by the ecclesiastics' love for Repository Art, and the sham Gothic or sham Classic which goes with it. We do not hold them to blame for their preferences. If there is question of any blame we only hold them to blame for their acquiescence in the rule of commerce under which we groan. A certain impudence in thus daring to cast blame upon men of God is not incompatible with a lively sense of our own sinfulness. But whereas the Confessional is adequate to our sins there is nothing adequate to deal with this iniquitous worship of commercial success and aggrandisement. "A man can be a very good Catholic in a factory." How true! But the fact remains that the factory-made art of the Catholic Repository is a very

II bad thing for making Catholics. If it be hard for a rich man to pass through the eye of a needle, it is no less hard for many men rich in culture[1] to pass through the door of a modern church. We know the answer well: a man must enter the Catholic Church in spite of all that ecclesiastics say or do, and stay there in spite of them. Nevertheless, it remains hard for many sensitive souls, sensitive *minds*—for soul is mind, and mind is intellect as well as will.

But again we say we are not complaining of the ecclesiastics' lack of culture—we do not advocate the æsthetic education of the clergy any more than of bankers. We are even willing to continue our present practice of hiding our best works when the parish priest comes to tea.[2] We do not demand that a priest should know a good thing when he sees it. We only ask that he should see that there is an application, an inevitable application, of Catholic faith and morals to the work as well as to the life of our time. Commercialism, industrialism, mass production are æsthetically degraded and degrading—that is *our* business. That they are ethically degraded and degrading is the clergy's business. To be a good Catholic in a factory is possible—just as possible as it

[1] "*Pulchritudinis studium habentes*"—Ecclus. 44.

[2] As a matter of fact, it is our wife who takes this tactful step.

is to be a good Catholic in a modern church, and just as difficult—the one because in it human responsibility is denied, the other because in it human intelligence and good sense are flouted.

But though as priest he is not, as man the priest is an artist, and saying Mass or Office is a work of artistry. And though as artist he is not, as man the artist is bound to be a man of prudence. There should not be, therefore, any abysmal lack of sympathy between them, at worst the quarrel should be a lovers' quarrel.

Under present conditions, with the abominable lack of responsible and intelligent workmen capable of supplying all that is necessary for the building and furnishing, still more the decoration, of churches, it is obviously necessary that the clergy should buy the products of commercial enterprise. The rule of reason, under such conditions, is obvious: Let things be plain, unadorned, undecorated, merely useful, efficient, hard, firm, and clear. Let us build churches as they build railway viaducts, with a strict regard to their structural utility. Let us apply the same rule to furniture and utensils and vestments, and let us leave out decoration altogether. Let us pay no heed to those who say that such churches will be cold and bare and dreary, and will drive the poor away. It is

II nonsense, anyway, and, even if it were not, it is an iniquitous suggestion that we buy cheap frippery to attract the poor. Even if it does attract them, that is not why it is bought. It would not be bought if the clergy disapproved of it.

Is it not odd that artists, who are accused of every sort of sensuality, should be in the position to preach asceticism and discipline to the clergy? Is it not odd that the clergy, who are accused of every sort of puritanism and other-worldliness, should be the most abject patrons of the loose and undisciplined and sentimental? It is not for nothing that plain serge is called "art" serge. It is because the really artistic thing is the thing devoid of the meaningless, the silly, the imitation, and, under present conditions, plainness is the only road to intelligence. Let a Catholic priest say he has no use for intelligence—let him say he only appeals to the emotions—we shall know what to reply.

III

TWOPENCE PLAIN, PENNY COLOURED

A PLAIN article costs more than a painted or decorated one. The reasons for this seem to be two. First: the normal human being likes things to be painted and decorated, therefore the demand for such things is large and their manufacture profitably organised in mass (mass production), and therefore they can be made cheap. Moreover, the competition between the sellers of such things is keen and their price kept low in consequence. Second: Bad or inferior materials and workmanship can be camouflaged by paint and ornament and bad or inferior material is cheaper than good.

It is obvious that thus the normal human notion of values is reversed—the simple has become the costly, the elaborate has become the cheap, and, as has been said, "it takes a complicated mind to live the simple life." It is also obvious that the human appetite for the painted and decorated is *normal* and that is the same as saying it is right. There is therefore no object in going against that appetite and, as in the case of "strikes" and "lock-outs," a man is not justified in embarking on a campaign unless there are reasonable grounds for hoping for success.

III Moreover, we have the honour to share the normal human appetite, in this as in other matters. Plain living with or without high thinking is very well as a policy of reparation, but it is no more normal to man than it is to any other animal. Are we not of more value than many sparrows, and does not God so clothe the flowers of the field that even kings have some difficulty in competing? Let it be clear then, not to say plain, that we hold no brief for plainness as such—except in thought and in speech.

On the other hand we have a prejudice in favour of good quality—especially in things that are not physically necessary.

We cannot live without bread or something of the sort (starch they call it), and therefore if we cannot get good bread we must perforce eat bad—provided it be good enough to eat—and so doing we sin neither against God nor our neighbour. The same applies to all things deemed necessary—from bread to tobacco, from sign-boards to C.T.S. tracts—if they be deemed really necessary, then we must have them, even though of inferior quality. "What is worth making is worth making badly" is a saying that contains this much truth: if a man needs it he must have it, however badly made. But if he need it not, if it be a thing supporting not his physical but his mental well-being, if it supply not a physical need but a mental, then there can be no sort of excuse if the thing be not made as well as it can be made according to our lights.

It may be urged that needs physical and mental impose the same obligation upon Christian men: that a badly made loaf is as much an evil thing as a badly printed book or a badly painted picture or a badly made face powder, and from the point of view of the producer this is true. A man who deliberately and not being under duress makes things less well than he knows how is a despicable creature and either fool or knave. It matters not whether the thing be bread or statues: the evil state of mind is equally abominable. But when it comes to buying things one has not made oneself it is different. Though the stomach, like the Kingdom of Heaven, is within you, it is fed on different food and the supply, in the case of the stomach, cannot always be obtained, as in that of the mind, direct from God.

If I can grow my own corn, grind my own flour, and bake my own bread, no doubt I shall be either fool or knave if I have anything but the best I can make. But if I am King of England or Cardinal of

Rome, I may not have time for farming, milling, and baking; I must perforce buy bread and must eat such as is set before me. I hold myself excused even if my stomach complain. The same reasoning does not apply to the things of the mind. I may hold that I need mental as much as physical nourishment—and I may be right. But whereas, unless I am farmer, miller, and baker, I cannot control my bread-making, there is no escape from blame if my *soul* is not nourished upon the best.

Good quality, then, in the things of the mind is of obligation, and of mental things it must be said that what is worth making *must* be made well—as well as we know how. And this applies not only to the high and lifted-up things called the fine arts—painting, sculpture, music, the drama, letters, architecture—it applies also to all those things which cannot by common sense be held to be strictly utilitarian—face and custard powder (except when ordered by the doctor), umbrella handles, frills and furbelows, and all ornamental things—these things minister to the dignity of humanity; they give that quality to life without which it is less worth living even for millionaires or mystics.

It is probable that all that we have so far written will be agreed to by most people. Few will claim that good quality in the things of the mind is not of obligation and everyone will agree that I must eat even if I cannot get good food. III

What is the reason, then, that things in churches, things (apart from pews and chairs) which obviously minister to mental needs alone—are usually bad? It cannot be that people deliberately do inferior work when it is church work; that people who buy things for churches deliberately buy what they know is bad. No, the reason is that people have a much lower standard of quality in ecclesiastical than in secular art. The ordinary standards of fitness which help to keep up a certain level of good quality are not applied to church building or furnishing. Critical reasoning is not applied to art—least of all to church art. Such standards as exist in the secular world are not applied in ecclesiastical matters. The standard of taste in the supply of objects for suburban drawing-room mantel-shelves is low, but not so low as that according to which statues and ornaments for churches are judged—nothing is quite so low as that. Chocolate boxes must at least suggest something sweet, and sweetness is not an evil thing. Drawing-room carpets and wall-papers sue for favour by an appeal to the love of bright colours and flowery fields—good things both, and if the standard of Tooting is low it is at least variable, and the best people in Tooting do at least imitate their betters in South Kensington. South Kensington has its eye on Chelsea, and Chelsea, as is well known, is the womb of art.

But Catholic Church art is not alive in that way. It is not, like the offerings at a harvest festival, an offering to God of the best fruits of human intelligence and labour. It represents not the best things people can produce, but simply what is conventionally considered to be the right thing, appropriate, that is to say, to an occupation (i.e. prayer) which has apparently nothing to do with the profession, business, or occupation by which people earn their livings. Church art, "devotional" art! The conventions of the drawing-room are dreary enough, God knows! but things no one would tolerate in the drawing-room are considered quite satisfactory in church. Why should there be such a difference of standard?

Even if we were wrong in supposing that the home standard is higher than the church standard—suppose it were the other way round—it would still be clear that there is a *different* standard, and that is the truth of the matter. There *is* a different standard; church and workshop have proceeded upon divergent paths for the last three hundred years and different standards of achievement have been set up in consequence. In the matter of painting, different aims have arisen, and what is considered good painting from a secular point of view is bad from an ecclesiastical. But the matter does not end there, for secular painting has got to greater heights in its own country than ecclesiastical painting in the ecclesiastical sphere; or rather, ecclesiastical painting has simply gone to the bad and good painting has become the more or less eccentric product of isolated individuals.

The reason for this is obvious. Painting, like all the other arts, is essentially a layman's job. The Church is dependent upon the secular world for the supply of all that pertains to the building and furnishing and decorating of churches.

The Church still needs the same kind of things as she has always wanted, but the world cannot and will not supply them except in the low and degraded form of the church furniture shop—"Repository Art." To produce any kind of good tradition requires generations of effort—such effort as can or will only be expended when the enthusiasm is intense and widespread. Intense and widespread enthusiasm is now alienated from the Church, and the

III Church, for her building and furnishing and decorating, must perforce depend for the most part upon those whose only interest is commercial.

What is produced simply in the way of commerce is inevitably inferior. What is produced in mass is obviously cheaper for the buyer and more profitable for the producer. But what is already inferior by reason of its purely commercial origin is made more inferior still by "mass" production.

The problem before us, then, is a difficult one. The Church needs things which intelligent artists cannot or will not supply. Why, in the absence of the work of intelligent artists, are church people, both clerical and lay, content with the degraded product of the worst kind of commercial enterprise? Why not have things "plain" if they cannot be got "coloured" and good?

We may take it that people will not have things plain because it is against nature—against human or any other kind of nature. We must take that for granted. It is no use at all expecting anything else.

The plain *as such* is not a better thing than the "coloured." Our preference for the plain thing amounts only to this: that in the absence of really good things the plain bad thing is less objectionable than the "coloured." But the instinct for decoration and colour and elaboration remains at bottom good and reasonable.

It may be necessary to "put the brake on" from time to time or all the time. Good taste is certainly mortified taste, and the best periods of artistic achievement are undoubtedly the more austere periods. But the present distaste of some people for the coloured and elaborate is not due to their austerity or mortification so much as to their right and proper loathing for the cheap and nasty and sentimental.

Certainly it would be very pleasant if our churches were denuded of all their present sacred images and pictures—if all their carving were carved off and all their windows filled with plain glass; but even then, though they would look better—they would look better than they are—it would only be a whitewashing of the sepulchre unless that iconoclasm were really the expression of the mind of the congregations.

The Church is not a cultured set and does not minister specially to the intelligent. Cultured people have got to take church-going as a penance ("for your penance go to the 11.0 Sunday Mass at —— Pro-Cathedral"), a well-deserved purgatory, a test of endurance.

III There is indeed no remedy while the buyers of church buildings and furniture are at the mercy of commercial enterprise.

You cannot expect poor people, lay and cleric, to give twopence for a plain thing which they can get for a penny "coloured," and you cannot expect a good workman or artist to make coloured for a penny what it costs him twopence to make plain. And, even were those difficulties to be overcome, there would still remain the fact that the modern artist, even when he has the understanding to produce the kind of building and furniture the Church needs, has generally no will to produce it and that few have even the understanding.

In general, then, there is clearly no remedy, and we must seek comfort in the two roads open to us. Wherever possible we must take the road to whitewash and carving off the carving, and wherever possible we must employ such good individual artists as are known to us. Moreover, we may take comfort in the fact that the superlatively nauseating quality of "Repository" Art, in spite of its cheapness, and the expensiveness of "Gothic and Classic," in spite of their sentimental attractiveness, are becoming "too much" even for the rank and file of the clergy and laity. Repository Art is very nearly as *démodé* as

Gounod. Architects are showing that grandeur of III
proportion and mass are obtainable in concrete and iron at half the cost of Gothic stonework. Perhaps we shall live to see the day when we may say again "penny plain—tuppence coloured."

IV

ART AND SANCTIFICATION

FIRST we must endeavour to see art in general perspective; for art is not merely here and now. The thing, whatever it is, goes back to the earliest beginnings of man's life. The distinction between art and fine art has not always been made, and has never been made clear, but that there is a relation between the two is certain, and it seems probable that the fine is always contemporary with the not fine. The making of objects for contemplation is no less natural to men than the making of objects for physical use, and "if man is essentially a tool-using animal, the tool is from the beginning that of the artist, no less than that of the labourer." [1]

Art is making in general—that is clear. The problem is not: What is art? but: Does it matter? And as nothing matters but the will of God, and as the will of God is "your sanctification," the question is: How does art affect man's sanctification?

It seems that, in a general way, there is no difficulty in considering any art which has a clearly utilitarian purpose. If you know what a thing is for, and if what it is for is good—i.e. in accord with good morals—then, without further ado, we deem the

[1] Dawson, *Progress and Religion*, p. 72.

thing good or bad simply because of its efficiency or inefficiency. A walking-stick is good if walking be good and the stick enable you to walk. A cooking-stove is good if cooking be good and the stove enable you to do it. A printed book is good if it be a good book and the print decently legible. In all such cases good is simply moral good and all such things are simply means to ends. They are good things if the end be good and they be efficient means to it.

But, from the earliest times, men have been more than merely moral and, in spite of the utmost endeavours of men of science and men of commerce and men of religion, it is extremely difficult to find objects of utility which are simply that and nothing more, or to find a workman whose concern with his work is merely that of its physical utility and efficiency.

This is what complicates the matter. If men made all things as they make corrugated iron, with no concern for anything but physical efficiency, then an enquiry into the "sanctification value" of works of art would be simply an enquiry into the moral values of things made, and such an enquiry might safely be left to bishops and princes, to the parish clergy and policemen.

But men do not work thus, and though in its

IV origin the word "art" means simply "skill," and though that meaning still attaches to it—indeed skill is the very body of all art works—yet, so common, so normal is it for man to concern himself with more than the moral value of his works, that the word "artist" has come to mean not simply "skilled workman" but "delightful" workman, and "work of art" means not "something skilfully made as a means to an end" but "something which is delightful as an end in itself."

God is the only being who is really an end in Himself. But things that are "godly" partake of His nature, and hence the enquiry into the value of works of art is simply an enquiry into their godliness in *themselves*. It is thus necessary to eliminate from the discussion all questions as to the physical or moral utility of such works. This elimination does not in the least imply that such questions are unimportant, but simply that they are irrelevant here and now. They are questions with which physicians and moralists are competent to deal. Our discussion is rather a matter of philosophy; for the love of wisdom is the love of things as seen in their ultimate causes, and God is the ultimate cause of all things.

We eliminate, then, all magical and utilitarian motives in works of art and retain for discussion simply the delectative, those motives which result in making a work of art delightful—delightful in itself.

Now this delight—is it of the mind or of the body or of both? The mind (intelligence, will), which knows, and the body (flesh and blood), by means of which we know, are the two components of man, spirit and matter, both real and both good. It is clear that the delight in works of art is of the mind. But it is the mind of man which delights, and man is spirit and matter. Mental delight is the object of art work, but, the avenue to that delight being the body, the body demands that the means shall be delightful also.

There is not necessarily any difficulty here. Though the flesh lusteth against the spirit, they are only enemies of one another in the same way as the innkeeper is the enemy of the traveller and seeks to delay him.

Appreciation is of the mind, the mind of man, the rational soul. Whoever knows what is appropriate to a rational soul will know what such a soul will properly find delightful. The delight of the mind is essentially a rational delight, and it consists primarily in the recognition of being. To the rational soul all being is delightful. But the beauty of God is the cause of all being; hence all being is beautiful, and hence the saying that the beautiful thing is that which being seen pleases—*id quod visum placet.*

We have said that art is primarily skill, but that it has come to mean delightfulness in things made—that quality in things made which renders them delightful to the mind which sees them in themselves, apart from or in addition to their magical or utilitarian purpose. But there are other modern definitions:

"Art is the expression of emotion," said Tolstoy.

"The business of the artist is to find a form to fit an emotion"; and

"The question is not what a work of art represents but what it makes you feel," says Mr. Clive Bell.

In all these modern definitions there is a harping on the words "feeling," "emotion." Hence the frequency of the phrase "art is self-expression," and hence, easily enough, art is not only the expression of the artist but also the response of the beholder. "Architecture," said Walt Whitman, "is what you do to a building when you look at it." It is difficult to say what precisely an artist intends to convey; it is perhaps less difficult to say what effect his work has upon us. Hence the notion that art has no objective reality; it is simply my feeling or yours. In fact, according to such notions God is something in ourselves making for righteousness and art is something in ourselves making for delightfulness.

Now all this art nonsense is perfectly all right if we realise that it is simply attempts to get at the truth and do not imagine that the truth has been got at. The crude utilitarian and sentimental notions of art leave so much out; the moral and didactic notions of art put so much in that it is not surprising that artists and critics have sought refuge in subjective emotionalism. On the one hand we were told that a work of art was simply something usefully well made or something which looked exactly like something else; on the other, that the whole business of the artist was to interpret the universe and thus to elevate and instruct the beholder. On the one hand we were made pawns in a game of commercial aggrandisement ("The Art School should be a centre to which the manufacturers may flock in the confident belief that they will find there guidance to enable them to introduce into their processes such a measure of art as would make their products more acceptable," said Sir Lawrence Weaver); on the other we were placed on pedestals and regarded as seers.

Making things delightful does indeed make them

saleable. In the discovery of what is delightful the artist is indeed a seer. But giving things a saleable quality is not therefore the artist's business, and a pedestal, however suitable for a statue, is a bad resting-place for a workman.

The truth, as usual, is not a mean between these extremes but a combination of both. "Whatever can be thought is true," as Bosanquet said. Tolstoy is right, Mr. Bell is right; so is Mr. Roger Fry, and We also are right in saying that the artist's job is making things which are delightful to the mind.

Now what precisely is delightful to the mind? Let us make a list of more or less well-known Works of Art:

The Venus of Milo
The Sistine Madonna
Luke Fildes' "The Doctor"
"The Soul's Awakening"
King Charles in Whitehall
St. Paul's Cathedral
The Pyramid of Cheops
The Forth Bridge
The new concrete church at Bâle
Epstein's "Day" and "Night"
Van Gogh's "Yellow Chair"
Matisse's Turkish Girl
The Cave paintings of Ajanta
Idols from Timbuctoo
The Dead March in "Saul"
Plainchant
Waterloo Bridge
Wagner's "Tristan"
The Queen Victoria Memorial
Modigliani's portraits
San Clemente (Rome)
Leonardo's "Joconda"
Stanley Spencer's "Resurrection"
Cezanne's Landscapes
Ming, Tang, or Sung pots
The Book of Kells
Gounod's "Ave Maria"
Joyce's "Ulysses"
The Morte d'Arthur
"Lead Kindly Light"

"Job" by Blake or by Job	Renoir's "Parapluies"	IV
The Wertheimers by Sargent	The Tale of Genji	
The Chef by Orpen	The Ballad of the White Horse	
The Song of Solomon	Love and Mr. Lewisham	
Bacchus and Ariadne by Titian	Moby Dick	
The Nave of Gloucester	Eros in Piccadilly	

Most of these works of art are well known. Probably half of them were "done to order." All of them are delightful to some people. All of them have either great moral value or great physical utility, but that is not what makes them delightful, though a knowledge of their moral value or physical utility may in some cases be contributive to our delight. What is their delightfulness? Their beauty is their delightfulness—*species eorum* —their very being.

And in what does beauty consist? Unity, proportion? But these are empty words; unless we know what it is that is to be unified, what proportions a thing ought to have. Clarity? But how can we delight in clarity if it be not clear to us? What is radiance to the blind?

We said all of these works of art are delightful to some people; but to some people some of them are not at all delightful. Who is right? How can we judge? Must we follow our fancy? The answer is, "Yes, but fancy is not necessarily blind." We are not speaking of moral or physical values. We have eliminated them from the discussion. There is no difficulty about *them*. If a picture or a book is an occasion of sin to one or to many, such picture or book can be destroyed "by the authority of the prince," and if prudish princes destroy good works no artist need worry—there are more fish in the sea than ever came out. No, the question here is not as to what is morally good or allowable, but as to what is intellectually recognisable and delightful, and in this matter the just man may follow his fancy. All that he need concern himself about is his justice. The intelligence is no less amenable to training than the will. The appreciation of the beautiful is the appreciation of the rational. It is the appreciation of what properly belongs to a rational soul. But this appreciation is not by a process of ratiocination; it is by sensibility —not the sensibility of the Sensitive Plant, but that of the spiritual man. Ratiocination is not therefore useless, but its use is chiefly negative—to weed out the irrational and to explain things, if that be possible, to less sensitive people.

We are not going to attempt any explanation here. It is not our business to say why this or that particular work of art is good or bad. Our business is simply to affirm that it is in function of their rational souls that men appreciate beautiful things; that when we are confronted by the situation wherein a certain thing which delights us is abhorrent to our neighbour, all we can do is examine our conscience and attempt to discover wherein our delight resides. Is it derived from sentiment, or from sensuality, from appreciation of the thing's usefulness, or from appreciation of the thing itself—the thing *seen*? None of these derivations is bad, but one or other may become insubordinate. The good painter is not devoid of sentiment or sensuality; nor is he scornful of usefulness. But first of all a painting must look like paint and a stone carving like stone. Music whose chief claim to delightfulness is its imitation of birds singing may be delightfully intriguing, but it is not the thing that music can do best. A painting which looks like a hole in the wall through which we may see a doctor counting a child's pulse is more of a curiosity, however pathetic, than a painting—in fact, it does its best not to look like a painting at all. If the Mother of God is to be thought of primarily as a buxom Italian woman with a rather noble-looking baby, then we are greatly indebted to Raphael. If we desire to have recorded in felicitous rhyme the tragic finitude of the human mind, then we are much indebted to Newman—as indeed we are; but it makes a bad congregational song. If we want to see what a family of wealthy Jews look like, then we are greatly indebted to Sargent. If our idea of nobility is inseparable from Doric columns, then Waterloo Bridge will seem the best bridge in London and the chain bridge at Chelsea the worst. If the memorial to Queen Victoria does not seem to us vulgar and absurd, then St. Clement's Church at Rome will leave us cold. If we like "Repository Art" we are bound to hate Negro idols. If we like the swelling notes that proceed from prima donnas' bosoms and think them an appropriate accompaniment to the Liturgy, then we can hardly be expected to appreciate the plain chant.

Modern art—the sort called Modern to indicate its mentality rather than its date—is in full reaction against the sentimentality and hypocrisy, the utilitarianism and smugness of the nineteenth century. In Victorian times art meant almost nothing but sentiment—Luke Fildes and Marcus Stone were Royal Academicians—if a painting had any quality as a piece of paint it was accidental. To-day among "Modern" painters it is the sentimental that is accidental. They are now concerned with the objective qualities of works of art, and primarily with the mental objectivity rather than the physical. The reasons for this are fairly clear and are mainly two: the reaction is against Victorian sentiment, that is, against Victorian mentality—hence modern artists are chiefly interested in æsthetic significance, and that is a thing of the mind; but—and this gives us the second reason—if modern artists are in revolt against Victorian sentiment, and this sentiment still persists among the masses of those who look at pictures and sculptures and, as far as the majority of the buying public is concerned, may therefore be called contemporary sentiment, then it follows that modern artists will find very little employment—the bulk of their work will be, as it is, done merely to please the artist himself. The modern artist is therefore divorced from architecture, from building, from house decoration, from furniture—from all those things which force him to have concern for the physical objectivity of art works. Hence it is only rarely that any attention is paid to the physical "finish" of a work of art. This makes the breach between modern artists and the general public even wider; for good workmanship, "trade finish," neatness, and what some painters scornfully call "tightness," are things naturally delightful, other things being equal. But it is just the other things that are not equal. So the ordinary philistine gets nothing—

neither things that he can understand nor things that at least seem to him well done.

Modern art is in revolt against Victorian mentality; what is its own mentality? Apart from the general enthusiasm for objectivity and detestation of illusionism and representation and anecdotage, there is of course no one binding idea among modern artists. How could there be unless they were all Catholics or all Baptists or all Hyperborean mystics? But there is perhaps one tendency more noticeable than others, and that is the tendency to return to primitive and elemental ideas. This is seen in the current enthusiasm for negro sculptures—an enthusiasm which reflects, on the higher plane of intellectual things, what, on the lower plane of physical enjoyment, is reflected by jazz music. But the interest in primitive sculptures is not the only form of the revolt against worn-out sentiment. Any kind of elemental thing seems preferable to the dead and by now stinking frowziness of sham Gothic and sham Classic romanticism. And the elemental is not by any means the coarse or uncouth or even simple. Form and colour in primitive paintings and sculptures are far more refined than in the popular works of the nineteenth century, more subtle, more sensitive; and as, in addition to their physical beauty, they represent ideas and notions of primary importance, it is not surprising that they are now objects of veneration to young men and women for whom Rodin is something of a mountebank.

Religion is the binding force of humanity. The history of cultures is the most important kind of history. While the modern world thinks that religion is a matter of opinion and history primarily a matter of biology there is not likely to be a reconciliation between modern art and modern life. This is all as it should be; the only regrettable thing is that the Catholic clergy are on the whole unsympathetic if not actually antagonistic to modern art. It is easy enough to understand this—just as it is easy enough to understand a poor man's succumbing to the temptation to steal money—but that does not make it right. Art is not the clergy's business; but religion is, and it is primarily a religious movement that modern art exhibits. It is a movement away from frivolity and hypocrisy and flattery and the worship of mammon.

Speaking of some modern wood-engravings by a Benedictine nun, the present Pope is reported to have said that he wished modern artists would "leave religion alone." But religion is just the one thing that cannot be left alone. It was false religion that created

IV Victorian sentiment; it is in their attempts to discover and make manifest true religion that modern artists are chiefly to be praised. With the clergy against them, they are bound to flounder in morasses of eccentricity.

V

ARCHITECTURE AS SCULPTURE

(Notes of a Lecture delivered to the Liverpool Architectural Society on 21 November, 1928)

ARCHITECTURE in particular defined as :

House building with an eye to beauty.

A beautiful thing is that which, being seen, pleases.

House = house, workshop, factory, church, town hall, etc.

Sculpture in particular defined as:

Carving or modelling of the human figure with an eye to beauty.

Architecture in general defined as:

(Distinguished from mere building.)

The putting together of different kinds of works into a co-ordinated whole, by a ruling mind, such that the parts, though retaining their several functions and identities, are merged in a unity by the design of the architect, i.e. master of the works. The *ruling motif* of the architect is thc making of a beautiful building or construction.

Sculpture in general defined as:

1. Differing from architecture in that the sculptor is only concerned with one kind of work,

V whereas the architect is concerned to co-ordinate many different kinds.

Both are concerned with beauty.

Both are concerned with things in three dimensions.

Both are concerned with the ordering of parts into a unity.

Both are generally concerned with service, i.e. making something useful.

Both endeavour to escape this concern.

2. Also sculpture differs from architecture in that, in architecture, construction, putting different things together, is essential; in sculpture it is not.

3. Also architecture differs from sculpture in that whereas the sculptor is thought of as doing the work with his own hands, and very often he actually does so, the architect is thought of as doing the work by means of other people's hands—he is co-ordinator of other men's work rather than executant of his own.

Beauty—the word is a stumbling-block.

Do not let us stumble over it.

Beauty is the *Splendour of Being*. The primary constituent of visible Being is Order.

Beauty in architecture is conspicuous order

—order shining out. Hence it is of the mind. It is the mind that is pleased by things called beautiful. (The kinds of pleasure which are not primarily of the mind are generally called *lovely*, because lovable, i.e. desired and desirable, satisfying a physical need or appetite rather than a mental.)

But the lovely and the beautiful are mixed—because man is matter as well as mind—both real and both desirable—both true and both good.

Hence man's work is concerned with both the *beautiful* and the *lovely*.

But art is specifically concerned with the beautiful—that is its ratio—its *raison d'être*—its reason of being.

Beauty—conspicuous order.

The beautiful—conspicuous order in things.

Order—rightly ruled, governed, arranged, proportioned.

Rightly—in accordance with the demands of mind.

Mind—*intellect*, i.e. the faculty of knowing, and *will*—i.e. the faculty of reaching out to things, grasping them, acting, ordering, governing in accordance with what is known.

When a thing is well made, well ordered, the mind

of him who contemplates it is at rest, is satisfied —is pleased.

This pleasure is not of the senses—though the senses share it.

Nor is it the pleasure of knowing.

It is not simply that kind of pleasure which we have when we discover the right solution of a problem.

Nor is it simply that kind of pleasure which we have when we see or receive an act of kindness.

It is the delight of the mind in seeing the thing itself.

It follows immediately upon the mind's grasping or comprehension of the thing presented to it.

It is the result of the mind's recognition of what is after its own kind.

In things of beauty the mind comes into its own.

It is possible to ask: What is a beautiful *building*?— but it is not possible to answer.

It is like asking: What is a beautiful animal, or what is a beautiful colour, or what is a beautiful shape?

It is necessary first to know what the thing is.

When we say, e.g. the Venus of X is a beautiful sculpture, we mean it is a beautifully sculptured Venus. Our knowledge of what the thing is is taken for granted. V

And in sculpture, as in architecture, the wider and deeper the knowledge the better.

But this knowledge does not signify book learning. It is more like the knowledge of friends—as who should say: Do you know Brown? To which the answer might be: Yes, I know him very well.

When we say, e.g. The Post Office at X is a beautiful building, we mean it is a beautifully built Post Office. Knowledge of what the thing is, is taken for granted.

The wider and deeper the knowledge of things, the wider and deeper are our powers of finding beauty—or the lack of it.

Men who have narrow and shallow views as to the nature of Post Offices will build Post Offices less beautifully than those whose views are wider and deeper.

Historically: sculpture comes first; architecture last.

Whatever view we take of early human history, it is obvious that making individual things comes

V before the job of construction and before the job of co-ordinating the labour of different kinds of workmen.

Cave man with bone—the type of human artist.

That is the workman making a thing as well as he knows how and as well as he can.

Making a thing—i.e. not a picture of a thing —not a representation.

Hence, generally, a thing of three dimensions, and a thing in three dimensions is a work of sculpture.

Whatever view we take of the physical origins or development of men and animals, it is clear that there is a being called man—even if only a creature of the imagination. Even if I only imagine it—still I do imagine it—there is in my mind an image called man, and this creature (imaginary or otherwise) is one for whom beauty is the first need, not the last.

This is true of the most primitive conditions. In fact, the more primitive the conditions the truer it is—so true that there are in such circumstances no lectures about it and no architectural societies. Man has not risen from depths of gluttony and avarice to the heights of beauty and disinterestedness in which we now find ourselves . . . rather it is that gluttony and avarice have overwhelmed him until he now finds himself in London or Liverpool. V

The sculptor is the type of the responsible workman.

The architect is the type of the responsible overseer.

In the absence of machinery and subdivided labour:

In the absence of commercial insubordination:

In the absence of cheap drawing-paper (it is often forgotten how dependent we are upon paper; imagine Wren's "detail" paper!) most workmen were responsible persons.

The sculptor, particularly so called, was one of a gang of responsible workmen whose work was co-ordinated by the architect.

To-day the sculptor, in the particular sense, is the only member of the gang who retains full responsibility—the others are only morally responsible for doing what they are told: they have no intellectual responsibility.

Consequence: The sculptor out of place on modern buildings. His work incompatible in kind with that of other building operatives.

Best architects admit this conclusion and leave out all carving and ornament—plain building.

In consequence: the architect's job ceases to be the co-ordination of the works of other responsible

V persons. He ceases to consider the building gang as *collaborating* with him.

Architect and contractor alone remain, all other men are mere hands.

Architect intellectually responsible for design.

Contractor morally responsible for execution.

Consequence: Architect set free from shackles of old building conventions—"styles" of architecture—"orders"—and free from all old architectural "properties," pillars, porticoes, capitals, cornices, arcades, flutings, rustications, etc. Exigencies of use on one hand and his own formal predilections on the other alone concern him—*and the latter are the ruling motives.*

The shape of the building when done has always been his chief concern—and the chief concern of the man in the street, too; but now that shape is not conditioned either by the wills of his employees or by the conventions of previous practice.

The architect is free to consider his building precisely as a sculptor considers his piece of stone—as a thing of mass in three dimensions, known to him by means of light and shade and colour alone. (The sculptor has the sense of touch also, but the architect deals with things too big to feel.)

Again: a man who shapes a thing to his liking with his own hands, alone or in collaboration with a few responsible and sympathetic assistants, is in a very different situation, with regard to the work, from that of an architect who shapes nothing with his own hands and cannot be said to collaborate with anyone.

At the best the architect is the more or less benevolent despot who nominates the contractor, and the contractor is in the position of employer to a gang of more or less unwilling slaves. They are not called slaves because they are paid . . .

Consequence: the best modern buildings may, from a reasonable distance, appear to be very great and beautiful works; but "close-ups" kill them—or, rather, show how dead thcy already are.

Design may be admirable—the execution being the work of machines is bound to be dead and dull and therefore not pleasing when seen.

V This state of things is unavoidable at present. The artist, whether sculptor or architect, is not a social reformer; he is bound to take things as he finds them.

At the present time we find responsible and intelligent and enthusiastic workmen are very scarce, so that for works of large size we are forced to employ mere *hands*—there are not enough *men*.

Consequence: if we are wise we shall either confine ourselves to such work as we can do by ourselves alone (or with one or two assistants)—i.e. we shall be sculptors . . . or, if "working with our hands" be not in our line, if our enthusiasm lies in the direction of constructing and co-ordinating, we shall become architects or engineers and confine ourselves to the construction of such works as do not call for anything but obedience from our employees.

An engineer's enthusiasm is confined to the work of construction—to the work of constructing something which will do something—as a bridge to carry a road, a dam to stop a river, a machine to sew on buttons. In no case is the engineer as such concerned with the beauty of the thing constructed. An engineer

> is a man who makes things worth using—an architect is one who builds things worth looking at as well as worth using. V
>
> Many works of engineers are worth looking at, but that is not what the engineer thinks they are for. Many works of architecture are worth using (living in, for instance), but that is not what the architect is chiefly proud of—nor is it that by which he is remembered.
>
> Who cares now whether the aqueduct at Nîmes ever held or ever could hold water?

As animals labouring under the necessities of eating and drinking, of shelter and communication, we are all interested in the usefulness of things, and a certain zest is given to our interest in things when we know "how they work"; but that is only because man is the most ingenious of animals; it is no indication of his superiority to the beasts that perish. What places him as lord of creation is not his cleverness or ingenuity, not his power of ratiocination, not even his perseverance or his courage. His claim to superiority is based solely on his power of contemplation; he alone of terrestial beings is able to recognise *being*; he alone is capable of disinterestedness. "Adam sinned when he fell from contemplation."

V And as the created universe is primarily a work of art and not primarily a work of kindness (that is why praise comes before thanksgiving and art is metaphysically above prudence), so works of art are more essentially human than works of usefulness or even than works of kindness (hence the "Humanities" does not mean Ethics but Arts).

These things being so, it is easy to understand the fascination of the modern architectural opportunity and its danger. Not for 300 years has architecture been so intellectually free, but neither, on the other hand, has it for 300 years been so lacking in support from high places. The highest service the enlightened architect can render is a service to shopkeepers and insurance societies. All other opportunities are denied him.

The churches and public authorities are not hidebound by utilitarianism, but they are hidebound by the fetish of style and are devoid of courage. (I speak of England. In France and Germany and other parts of the Continent they dare to put up frankly modern churches—e.g. the church at Le Raincy, near Paris.)

The enlightened sculptor is in a worse predicament. There is no place for him on building—he is no longer a normal part of the building gang. He is dependent upon the connoisseur, and his place is now the museum.

I am not here to speak for sculptors, nor am I concerned to decry museums. My thesis is simply this: that architecture under modern conditions is rightly to be thought of as sculpture. Sculpture is no longer a thing applied—if you have money enough. The sculptor is no longer one of the people your architect naturally calls in. The only sculptor employed in building work is the architect himself. The building as a whole is a piece of sculpture, and any detail or part is a detail or a part of a piece of sculpture. The steel framework is precisely the armature; the stone or concrete is the modelled body.

You may say, "Yes, but that has always been so. Good architects and builders have always so regarded their job." That is true. But whereas in former times—before industrialism entirely dehumanised the workmen and divorced the artist from the building gang—the building as a whole was a work of sculpture and each individual part was also the work of responsible workmen, i.e. artists; now the architect is the one remaining artist engaged in building. The result is clear and yet few see it.

Imagine a sculptor who has carved a grand monumental figure of a woman. He might say to himself: Now, what it needs is a delicately carved necklace. Ha! the very thing to employ that dunderhead Brown to do—he's got no ideas of his own, he'll do just what I tell him, he's frightfully skilful and absolutely dull and mechanical. In fact, I'll carve the figure and I'll get the necklace done by machinery.

Is such a soliloquy likely?

Take another case the other way round.

Imagine a sculptor who has designed a very simple figure—so simple that it is patent of precise measurement. He might say: Well, anyone, even that dunderhead Brown, can do accurate measuring. I'll let Brown hack out the figure but I'll carve the necklace myself.

On the face of it that soliloquy is more possible—but even so, our sculptor might have doubts and say to himself: No, old Brown's careful measurement will be quite unintelligent, the thing will be so damned insensitive that my pretty necklace will belong to another world. I'd better carve the whole thing myself.

Now, apply these things to the business of building. The architect cannot possibly build the whole thing himself—he is forced to employ a host of industrialised dunderheads. What, then, about necklaces—i.e. carved cornices, sculptured figures, and what not? Why, leave them out.

But there is another sort of danger confronting the intelligent and enlightened modern architect. It is a modern form of the danger of Baroque—the making of buildings which, while purporting to be churches, factories, or what not, are really only phantasies. The same danger confronts the modern sculptor. He may, if by strange chance he should get such a commission, be asked to carve a crucifix for a church, and being immersed in the problems of "significant form," he may make a thing which, however beautiful it may be when seen simply as a lump of stone, is in no proper sense a crucifix at all. If the thing is to be a crucifix, the nature of a crucifix must be treated with extreme respect. If it is to be a stone crucifix, the nature of stone must also be treated with extreme respect. The two extremes must be combined: that is the golden rule.

So with building—if it is a factory, a water tower, a bridge, the nature of these things must not only not be lost sight of, it must be treated with extreme respect. If the building is of stone or concrete or iron, the natures of those materials must be treated with extreme respect. Again, the extremes must be combined. And not only the nature of the building, the nature of its plan and construction also must be respected.

Some architects are so enamoured of what they call the vertical line—just as others are of what they call the horizontal line—that they will work in their precious vertical line whether or no. It is as though a painter who was enamoured of hair couldn't leave it out even in a painting of "My Julia's Leg." The citizens of London who, on account of the proximity of the Tower, insisted on the Tower Bridge being "Gothic," were guilty of the same kind of foolishness.

The architect to-day, then, is in a position which is both extremely strong and extremely unfortunate. His opportunities are unsurpassed. The immensities of scale should lead him to sublimity. Facilities of construction in iron and concrete, with the gigantic lifting powers of modern cranes, give him remarkable opportunity to model vast and impressive sculptures; for the architect-sculptor is a modeller, not a carver—his act is plastic rather than glyptic. But he suffers from two misfortunes, the one spiritual the other material.

1. The occasion of his labour is without spiritual significance. I am not here to preach religion. I simply state it as a fact, that commerce (even heightened by dreams of empire and universal brother-

hood), and domesticity (even without the degradation of birth control) are not powers that can move the mind of man to its highest, i.e. most characteristic expression. V

2. On the material plane he suffers the misfortune of having no sensitiveness in his fingers—i.e. the men who do the work, his "hands," are without feeling. What is measurable he can order and it will be done—what is not measurable—what depends upon the sensitiveness of the hand—he is entirely deprived of.

I repeat, I am not a social reformer or a preacher of religion. The artist must take things as they are. He is the realist *par excellence.*

I am not here to tell you what my job as a sculptor is under the circumstances. But being a sculptor, and architecture having become sculpture in a way entirely without precedent, I am able to speak to architects without presumption, and, paradoxical though it may be, it has become irresistibly clear that the architect, to get the best out of his job, has now got to eschew not only all the old business of the styles of architecture—that was worn to nothing a century ago—not only all the old architectural "properties"—pillars and capitals, cornices, pediments, and what nots—there is no one now to make them

V —he has got to eschew, resolutely, deliberately, all that has formerly been called sculpture.

Mass, proportion, scale, unity, light and shade and colour, and all these things springing naturally out of the very nature of the thing to be made, these things are for the architect as for the sculptor, the very stuff of his job.

From the Pyramid of Cheops to the bare interior of Westminster Cathedral (before they ruined it with marbles and mosaics) beauty and sublimity in architecture have never been dependent upon carving and ornament.

To-day, when such things as carving and ornament are not to be obtained (save as the rare product of individual artists whose connection with building is a mere fiction—a survival having no reality), it is more than necessary that architects should be independent of them.

This is no wail of despair. Facing the facts cannot be that.

On the contrary, it is essentially optimistic to suppose that the rule of reason can so far prevail.

It is simply unreasonable to bewail the present state of things.

Architects have got as good a chance of achieving purely architectural beauty as ever they have had, and if sculptors may legitimately grieve that building works no longer offer them opportunities worth having (and an architectural setting is the best opportunity for sculpture), even they may feel that the present state of things is not without its special advantages. A certain clarity, an increased disinterestedness, a certain emancipation is the prize of those who, cut off from the exigencies of utilitarianism and the need to placate the sentimentality of a mob fed on cinema and daily newspaper romance, pursue beauty as a hermit pursues sanctity.

There is one drawback to the plain building unadorned. That is, the man in the street doesn't like it.

But a wise artist is one who makes things people can like for the wrong reasons. Plain building is cheaper. Let the man in the street comfort himself with that.

VI

PAINTINGS AND CRITICISM (1930)

WHETHER wall pictures are or are not an essential part of interior decoration in the home has been well debated elsewhere. My business here is to carry the debate a step farther back. Barbarians or civilised, we all love pictures, but what is a picture that we should love it?

The National Gallery is always with us and so, as in the case of the poor, the attitude of the general public towards it is as cold as charity; but the exhibition of Italian pictures "now on" at Burlington House induces a warmer atmosphere for these debates. Moreover, as all the pictures come from one geographical area the problem is isolated; it is possible to survey the picture-making business from beginning to end with some approach to lucidity.

The main cause of difficulty is that the makers of works of art, whether ships, shoes, or painted pictures, are necessarily different people from those who write and talk about them. We have not only the producer and the consumer confronting one another; we have that third party, the interpreter, the go-between, the professional critic. And the critic has neither the responsibility of the maker of things nor the needs or appetities of the buyer or user of things. If he tends to portray the consumer's appetite rather than the producer's, nevertheless he remains irresponsible—he neither makes the thing nor pays for it.

Hence it is that the business of criticism tends to be merged in and befogged by the business of æsthetic theorising. The questions for the artist—what is a picture and how shall I make it?—and the questions for the buyer—what picture do I want and whom shall I employ to paint it?—are lost in the cloud of questions asked by the art critic—what do I like about pictures and why do I like it? Is art the expression of emotion? (Tolstoy), or the production of "significant form"? (Clive Bell). Is art the expression of truth in terms of beauty? (Herbert Read).

This state of affairs is, of course, the special affliction of the cultured classes. In the ordinary picture shop, in the Strand or in Hammersmith, they are not concerned with these burning questions. In such places pictures are bought and sold like any other furniture, and this is exactly how it should be. It is not the ordinary picture shop that is wrong. The goods sold may be poor and cheap, but they are bought and sold in the proper way of business like grocery or motor-cars.

Now this is an attitude of mind entirely foreign

and distasteful to the art critic. For him pictures are neither useful nor necessary—neither grocery nor furniture. However much he may talk about the mission of the artist to interpret the universe—and thus to take on the business of the philosopher and the seer—however much he may talk of the artist as an agent for the improvement of people's minds—and so a partner in the business of the moralist and the man of religion—he is really only interested—and rightly so because it is the only thing he can do which nobody else can do—he is really only interested in psycho-æsthetic analysis.

Now this, as I say, is all as it should be; that is, the art critic's business—very useful and interesting. But it is not the artist's business and it is not the buyer's business. For the artist pictures are things. For the buyer they are things. For the artist—that is to say, for the artist in general ever since the world began! You go to Lord Leverhulme for soap (if you like his kind of soap) and you to go to Sir John Lavery for portraits (if you like his kind of portraits). You buy Sunlight Soap because you imagine it will wash clothes. You buy Sir John Lavery's portraits because you want a portrait of someone, and you imagine that Sir John Lavery will do it well. You think you know when clothes are clean, and you think you know a good likeness when you see one. But in neither case are you concerned with any "Art Nonsense." You rightly and properly leave that to the critics, whose business it is.

Of course I am not denying that all sorts of high and subtle qualities may be found in both soap and painted pictures. The buyer whose mind is by nature or training both high and subtle will naturally discriminate between the less and the more clean, between the portrait which is merely photographic and one which has not only seized the character and quality of the sitter, but is also "significant" in form—whatever that may mean to him. But the point is that the basis of the business, both for the buyer and for the artist, whether discriminating or otherwise, is that the artist supplies a certain kind of manufactured article which the buyer has a need for.

If this still remains the basis of trading between artist and buyer among ordinary people, it has been woefully undermined among folk of the more consciously cultured classes, and here the faults are on all sides. It is not all the fault of the critic, though he has accentuated the evil. The spread of industrialism and factory production has brought it about that the arts called "fine"—picture painting and sculpture, music and letters—are the only arts in which the workmen engaged are responsible people and are treated as such. This makes painters and sculptors specially self-conscious and peculiar persons, and encourages in them the notion that it is their special and peculiar personalities which they are paid to express. A painting of a sunset or of the Blessed Virgin is no longer regarded simply as a good or bad painting of a sunset or of the Blessed Virgin, but as a good or a bad example of such and such an artist's manner. Industrialism has placed the artist on a pedestal; the artist finds it profitable to remain there, and the critic sees no other place for him.

But if industrialism has brought it about that the only responsible individual workmen are now those engaged in the "fine" arts—in all other arts workmen are little more than animated "hands" or tools—the notion of art which is the basis of the profession of art-criticism is a notion having an origin several centuries older than the industrial revolution. It may be said to have originated at the Italian Renaissance.

Before that Renaissance the business of art-criticism can hardly be said to have existed. You bought pictures as you now buy boots and shoes; you employed painters as you now employ builders and engineers. You compared one painter with another as being more or less efficient to supply the thing you wanted. You did not ask him to express himself any more than we ask a designer of submarines to express himself. The art of painting was the art of making things in paint. Some things are better made in paint than in stone or in tin. The function of criticism was to know precisely what one wanted and precisely whether one got it.

Before the Renaissance, man the painter was not an outsider who looked on the world and told you in paint what he thought of it, or how he felt about it. He was an insider—one of the gang of men who made things—a collaborator with God in creating. He did not say : " God made this thing and I am man enough to appreciate it and expert enough to express my appreciation." He said, in effect: "God made trees of wood and leaves; I make trees of paint. God made men of flesh and blood; I make them of coloured earth. Without me painted trees and men would not exist—any more than houses of stone or ships of iron. It matters little to me and still less to God what I think about the natural world. What matters to me and to Him is that I should be the vehicle, the appointed vehicle, for the continuation of creation. Paintings and sculptures, buildings and all things made, are as natural as blossoms on the rose."

VI As natural! But it is not natural for a painted man to look like a man of flesh and blood—the nature of paint is not that of flesh. After the Renaissance the tendency to naturalistic imitation, to the production of accurate representations of natural appearance, greatly increased; and it is notable that this increase was in exact relation to the emergence of the trader and merchant class from feudal bondage. Kings, princes, and governors were no doubt intrigued by it; ecclesiastical patrons were not averse to it; but the real spur to artistic anecdotage came from the uncultured newly rich, newly enfranchised, newly powerful bourgeois.

The Renaissance was not primarily the enfranchisement of the trader, but synchronised with it as it synchronised with the Reformation in religion. All these things together produced the new attitude of mind. The useful arts became more and more merely useful; the "fine" arts became more and more merely fine. Emancipated from the business of supplying goods to order, the workman became the artist; the workshop became the studio. In the course of time other workmen became factory hands—nothing to do with art—and the artist became the purveyor of sweetmeats—nothing to do with anything useful.

In this welter the profession of art-criticism grew VI
to importance. The banalities of the merely photographic and sentimental on the one hand and the high and subtle problems of æsthetics on the other, make it necessary that someone should exist who can be guide, counsellor, and friend to the unfortunate buyer torn between his carnal appetites and the yearnings of his soul.

Let us be quite clear about the point at issue. It is not at all that art-criticism is a useless or frivolous science. On the contrary, it is most important that in this matter, as in others, the truth be discovered, and among writers on art are many who have made valuable discoveries. It is not at all that the paintings of the post-Renaissance centuries are all frivolous or merely imitative and sentimental. On the contrary, from the fifteenth century up to our own days, hosts of great artists have painted hosts of great pictures—great in the sense that they exhibit qualities of mind and sense unsurpassed and perhaps unsurpassable by men. There is no question of the value of enlightened art-criticism or of the value of the works of men of genius from Raphael to Cézanne.

The point is simply this: that the tendency of art-criticism, in so far as it is accepted by artists and by buyers, is to obliterate the truth that, primarily, paintings are things like groceries and furniture—and thus both artists and buyers think of them when unsophisticated and not misled by æsthetic theory—and it is to confuse artists and buyers, but especially buyers, by giving undue prominence to the point of view of the looker-on—the person who neither paints pictures nor buys them—whose *raison d'être*, whose only excuse, whose only claim is that he can see more in a picture than the man who painted it.

"The artist does the work and the critic has the inspiration," and his inspiration is so intense that both artist and buyer are carried away by his enthusiasm. A painting of the Crucifixion ceases to be a painted crucifixion and becomes a symbol, not of Christianity, but of the artist's æsthetic idiosyncrasy. It is not that what the critic says is not true, but that it is a negligible truth, a misleading truth. Far better that painters and poets should think of themselves as grocers than that they should think of themselves as seers. Far better that they should join the ranks of the factory hands than that they should allow it to be claimed, as it is now being claimed, that industrialism, because it has made the making of useful things the affair of nincompoops and puppets pushing buttons, has set the artist free from the degradation of making anything useful.

Postscript

Although the artist is primarily a maker of things and only accidentally a prophet and a seer, or one who "leaves the world better than he found it," or the expresser of his own or other people's emotions, nevertheless, in his reaction against the academies, on the one hand, and the cult of æsthetics on the other, he must beware of taking part in what M. Julien Benda calls "the great betrayal." A publication of the British Institute of Industrial Art informed artists that at no time in the history of this country was it more necessary to "swell the volume of foreign trade," and that, to that end, the artistic quality of British goods must be improved. All patriotic artists . . . etc. But the artist's responsibility is to the thing he makes and to the person he makes it for—not to his country any more than to an æsthetic theory. If he refuses to take the point of view of the art critic, still less can he take that of politicians who are simply the mouthpieces of bankers and manufacturers interested in "big" business. The art critic seeks to place the artist in the skies; the politician would bury him under a mountain of mud, whereas it is necessary that he should keep his feet on the earth and his head above ground.

Therefore when I say: Better be a factory hand than agree that art is not concerned with anything useful, I do not at all mean that the artist should conceive of himself as helping to swell the volume of foreign trade, or as giving to mass-produced articles that "artistic" appearance which, coming from Manchester and Birmingham, they naturally lack. I mean simply that, as the beautiful is a sort of good and not a sort of truth, so works of art are a sort of goods and are not the product of a sort of psychological exhibitionism.

Things, things, things—things for use, things for delight, and things for fun; but anyway not things for boosting foreign trade.

VII
SCULPTURE AND THE LIVING MODEL

LET us try and be sure that we are all thinking of the same things and in the same way. In the broad sense sculpture is any thing made by men in three dimensions which is not made to serve a physical utilitarian purpose—a thing more delightful than useful—though delights have their use and uses are not without their delight. Thus a house is a thing made in three dimensions, but we do not call it sculpture, because it is not modelled or carved simply to produce a shape delightful to the mind of him who sees it, but is a thing constructed for the physical use of him who lives in it. But a mausoleum may be a work of sculpture, because a corpse is indifferent to its surroundings and the thing exists chiefly to satisfy the minds of those who look at it from the outside. Again, a walking-stick is not called a work of sculpture; but a sculptor may make a walking-stick in such a way that it will be a thing delightful to look at whether or not he or anyone else uses it to walk with.

And a thing may be a work of sculpture even if it be delightful only to madmen; for the nature of things is such that the object of the will is the good, and even madmen desire what seems good to them.

In the narrow sense, sculpture is the making of images, and it is with this business that I am here concerned.

The living model is, broadly, anything seen in nature; more narrowly it is the living human body. Again, it is with the narrow sense that I am here concerned. We have, then, the things called *Images* and the thing called the *human body*. The word image, curiously enough, for it is generally forgotten, means something imaginary, something seen in the imagination. It does not mean simply something seen in a mirror. The imagination is a faculty of the mind and the mind is very far from being simply a mirror. With great pain and labour the mind can be trained to act simply as a mirror, but it does not do it naturally or easily, though some people's minds do it more naturally and easily than others. Certain races of cave-men seem to have had minds of this kind, and they painted on the walls of their caves representations of things seen which are as accurate in their verisimilitude as anything done by the most highly trained students of our Art Schools. The mind which is merely a mirror is the really primitive mind. Hence the real "Primitives" are not the Pre-

Raphaelites, but the Cave-men and Royal Academicians. But generally and, as I should say, normally the human mind is not a mirror; it is a knowing and loving apparatus, and the faculty called the imagination is not so much concerned to create verisimilitudes as to create visions of what is known and loved. In the ordinary way, and speaking of men's works throughout the ages and not specially of men's works in Victorian England, men have not often been inclined to the mistake that a photograph of a thing seen was the same thing as a representation of what was knowable and lovable in it. Men have not generally been inclined to think that the production of illusion was the painter's or sculptor's chief business. They have generally been inclined to think of mimicry as a delightful but quite unimportant trade, a trade for mountebanks. To go on the stage and look exactly like Lloyd George and yet not *be* him is naturally a very attractive trick, and all kinds of impersonations and peep-shows and topical cinematography are amusing and instructive, but such things are not only not the best things men can do: they are not even the things men naturally want to do most. They do not want to do them most because, as it would appear, they are not the natural product of normal minds.

VII They are not the sort of images which the mind normally creates.

The knowing and loving apparatus which is the mind of man naturally cooks all that the eye and the ear present to it, manipulates it, distorts it if you like, alters it, fosters it, probes it, speculates upon it, thinks about it, chews it, sucks it like an orange and makes marmalade of it. The one thing it does not naturally do is make a verisimilitude of it.

It is true that some people and some races are gifted with the talent for seeing things as the camera sees them, and such persons or peoples enjoy great popularity. But this popularity is probably due to the rarity and peculiarity of such a gift and not at all to its being in any way specially a good gift or a venerable one.

If in the period which now seems to be drawing to its close the ability to see like a camera and draw like a photograph was considered to be the prime necessity for image makers, we must believe that something had gone wrong, that is to say, become abnormal in the minds of the people of that period. And this belief is very easily supported by evidence. The crown and summit of the intellectuality of the period was the discovery that man not only knew nothing for certain but was *unable* to know anything.

So much for the mind as a knowing apparatus! Who dared be anything but agnostic in those days? And the crown and summit of the morality of the period was a police-made internal peace and goodwill and a universal rule of international hatred, suspicion, jealousy, and war. So much for the mind as an apparatus for loving! Who dared be anything but militarist in those days?

And, to come down to lesser things, we must remember that the last four hundred years have been a period of "strict attention to business," to commercial expansion and the acquirement of riches. It is hard for a rich man to enter the kingdom of heaven, and it is hard for him to like anything but flattery, and of flattery imitation is the sincerest form. The whole period had been imitation—one vogue after another. Imitation Roman, then imitation Greek, then imitation Chinese, then imitation Gothic, and at the end the sculptor was expected to make imitation photographs.

Moreover, as the period progressed the working man became more and more the irresponsible tool of his employer. As the factory system developed the craftsman became more and more the mere "hand"—incapable of doing anything but what he was told. In such a period, and especially towards its close, and in spite of the presence of eccentric individuals of exceptional intelligence and sensibility, the mind of man in general naturally decayed—became abnormal and diseased. The factory hand is not expected to have a mind; he is not expected to know anything, and love among the machines is obviously out of place. The development of the imagination was out of the question. The word itself became a reproach; to call a person imaginative was, as near as no matter, to call him an idiot.

In such a period, in such circumstances, therefore, it was inevitable that it should be thought that the first thing to be attained by the image maker was likeness to nature—to imitate Nature, not "by working as she works," but by producing the appearance which she produces. All other images are too difficult; they imply too much. They imply a knowledge which is more than that obtained by measurement and a love which is more than the love of one's fellow-men. At enmity with all this, then, we may lay it down that the thing called an image is an original product of the mind, of the mind informed by life and work, by a life and work which involve intellectual as well as moral responsibility. It is the product of knowledge, not merely of information, and of love, not merely of comfortable acquaintance.

We make images out of what we know, not merely of what we can copy by looking. We make images out of what we love, not merely of what is seductive or of what has seduced us. VII

Such is the image in the mind, and it is the image in the mind which is the object of the image maker or sculptor. The stone carving or clay model is first of all in the mind; it is carved or modelled in the mind before it is carved or modelled in stone or clay. Of course seeing is a necessity, for, as things are for men, nothing is in the mind but comes to it through the senses, but the presence of images in the mind is not only the result of seeing but also, and more important, of thinking, willing, and loving.

And, obviously, the importance of the image made is relative to the importance of what the sculptor knows and of what he loves. But do not let us be misled by the title in the catalogue. Because a man carves a crucifix it is not proved that he either knows or loves God. Because a man paints a cottage chair it is not proved that he only knows the niceness of porridge and eggs and bacon. Nevertheless in the course of human history it is clear that the great periods of image making have in fact been those wherein the ruling power in men's minds was religious, and that it is only the irreligion of our time which compels painters and sculptors to seek in common objects for the knowledge and love of God which church people seem to have lost. It is not the fault of the painters and sculptors if, until quite recently, the chief function of the churches seemed to be the fostering and blessing of commercial aggrandisement. Their "good old German God" was no worse in this respect than He who was supposed to guide the fortunes of Christians in England and America, whether C. of E. or Nonconformist.

I say the importance of the image is primarily the importance of what it signifies, but in the making of the image, in its material embodiment, there emerges another importance: namely, the importance of the image as a material thing. It is no longer merely an idea in the mind. It is a thing in this world, in this England, in this town, in this wall, in this stone. Did it exist as it should exist in the mind of him who knows and loves and, now, does it exist as it should exist in this place, in this stone? Was it as it ought to be in the mind; is it as it ought to be in the stone? For as the mind has its rights and wrongs so has the stone or the clay or the bronze. What may be right in the mind may not be right in flesh and blood, and what may be right in flesh and blood may not be right in stone. And what may be wrong in one may be right in another. So there is conflict, and give and take, and a sort of marriage.

We hold, then, that things exist in flesh and blood and these things are received into the mind, and there they are dwelt upon and transformed into creatures more suitable to that mental habitation than things existing in ponderable flesh can be. And because these creatures of the mind are the fruit of love and there is "great joy at their making—they are not begotten betwixt sleep and wake"—because of this love we turn again to the fleshly world, the world of stone and wood and clay and metal, and recreate the mental image, make it manifest, communicate it. This is the way the common works of art are made—the way they have been made for a million years—the way they are always made where the mind is not tired and decayed. The sculptor is not a person who is born with the knack of making clay look like flesh and blood, who knows by nature or by training all the tricks which are useful for producing an illusion, who knows or has learnt all the muscles of the body and their funny names and can put them into his figures—all in their right places. There are such sculptors and they have their proper and honourable uses—in a surgeon's anatomy school or a museum of natural history. There are such sculptors, but they are only a small side department. The main body of artists, as we may see from the works they have left —from the most ancient Egyptian and Peruvian to the latest Indian bazaar carvings and South Sea Island and Negro idols—are recreators of *mental* images. And, in the process of recreation, reference to the living model is rarely made. It is not at all that the work is "done from memory," as we say; it is recreation not recollection. It is not a memory of what you saw but a copy of what you actually see—*in the mind* —a copy, but also a translation—a translation from the terms of mentality to those of material. And therefore you must know the language, its spirit, its "genius" as they call it. You cannot, except as a joke, say *je ne pense pas*, or *non puto* to mean "I don't think." Some images are not translatable into stone but only into bronze or brass. Some images are not translatable at all. In any case the reference is from the stone to the mind and not from the stone to the living model. "Art lives entirely on the side of the mind."

The training of artists, therefore, is twofold. First, there is the training of living. The child brought up in a dark cellar or in an art school will know nothing of humane life. Art training is first of all the training obtained by living the ordinary life of the time. Thus the mind is nourished on reality and not romance. Things are made for the life of the world—they are made to sell; they are sold because people want them enough to buy them. Buying means paying money, which means bread and butter. People who sell sculptures get bread and butter in exchange and justice demands an exact equivalent. If we take bread and butter from those who make it, we must give in exchange what those who make bread and butter want. We must in justice be part of the life of our time. We cannot sit apart and demand food in return for what the baker and the butcher do not want. If we can make nothing which our fellow-men desire to have, then, in justice, we should, like hermit saints, go out into the desert and only eat what we can find. The alternative is to live the parasitic life of those who depend on the favour of wealthy connoisseurs and art dealers whose chief concern is to create a vogue for our work on account of its peculiarity and to create a scarcity of value. And the artist who elects to live thus will become a kind of connoisseur himself—a connoisseur of emotions, of the colours of factory smoke, a connoisseur of things of value only in the studio—funny things like "formal values," "tone values," the "relations of masses."

VII He will be in great danger also of becoming a sort of prostitute, a sort of courtesan, a sort of lap dog, a person existing only for the pleasure of his patrons. And he will live in a world of unreality. He will think of himself as a sort of seer or mystic for whom the common life of work, and working hours, is not good enough—an insult to his superior gifts. His life will be a conglomeration of loose living and spiritual pride. And by loose living I do not mean simply "immoral" according to the standards of stock-brokers and Victorian spinsters; I mean a real untidiness and formlessness leading to complete dissolution. And by spiritual pride I do not mean that sense of one's own rightness which made a man like Bl. Thomas More prefer martyrdom to royal favour; I mean spiritual insolence, interior self-sufficiency.

And there is an even worse aspect of this freedom, this isolation of the artist from common life and necessary work. The saying that "Industrialism releases the artist from the degradation of making anything useful" has a terrible sting in it. It is, in reality, the freedom of Sodom and Gomorrah. Imagine those cities of æsthetes. Cities full of art schools—where men and women make the gestures of love but bear no fruit; where wine is continually poured out but never drunk; where meat is tasted but not eaten. All is taste, the best taste. And all this, not on account of some exculpating economic circumstance, such as that which makes "birth-control" among the poor forgivable if not excusable, but on account of a false mysticism—an attempt to behave as spirits while still inhabiting bodies—and all with an air of emancipation from the narrow-mindedness of Puritans but, in reality, sheer puritanism. The "degradation" of making anything useful—the "sordidness" of child-bearing—the "mere animality" of digestion—such are the phrases of Sodom and Gomorrah. Such are the phrases of æsthetes, and they disclose the root ideas of puritanism. Matter is not good enough for man. "Sculpture," says a well-known exponent of the art, "is the relations of masses"—just *is*. Marriage, say the æsthetic contraceptionists, is the relations of bodies—just *is*. Food is taste—just *is*. I reply, sculpture *involves* the relations of masses; marriage *involves* the relations of bodies; food *involves* tasting; but none of these things is *merely* relations—*simply* relations—relations isolated from context.

On the other hand, you must not suppose that I am denying to painters and sculptors the privilege of poets—the privilege to reach out in their art beyond the confines of merely human service to regions of mystic spirituality as pure as their necessary dealings with letter and sounds will allow. Let all who will go this road. But it is the road of saints and cannot be paved with either gold or bread and butter. There can, indeed, be no true mysticism without asceticism. "The greatest danger" is "not from matter and spirit, but from a would-be religion and a would-be spirituality," says the sage. But, he adds, in the saints we see "harmonised" with "an audacious movement towards pure spirit," "a modest and cheerful submission to the necessities of human nature."

Secondly, the training of the artist is the training of making things in the actual material of which they are made—not designing things on paper for other people to engrave by photography, not designing things in clay for other people to copy in stone or bronze, but doing the actual engraving, stone carving, or bronze founding and chasing.

The first training—that of living, fills the artist's mind with ideas and images, with things that he comes to know, with things to fall in love with. He may learn philosophy and gain religion—that is to say, the experience of God.

The second training—that of making things as they are used in the world, will teach him, if for instance he is a sculptor of stone, what stone is actually like, what can and cannot be done in it, what are its special qualities, what it lends or gives itself to best. Also he will learn what things are wanted, the conditions under which they are made, the places they are made for, the cost of materials and labour, and the prices of things when made—the whole collection of factors, and things otherwise unknowable.

And in neither of these trainings is there the thing which is called "life study" or "the life class" or "drawing from the life," because drawing from life does not really come into the affair—generally speaking. Drawing from the life and the special study of anatomy is a special art, or rather there are several special arts which require "life study" for their perfectioning. Thus the engraver of plates for surgical and anatomical textbooks must study the thing of which he is to make engraved diagrams. And portrait painters and sculptors who do portraits must at least see their sitters and study the disposition of bones and flesh—though, even for them, the thing is better learnt on the job, in the workshop, from the actual sitter, than from hired models in art schools. For portrait painting is, like tombstone making, a thing, a trade having a real attachment to life, and is not an academic subject like the study of Greek antiquities.

VII The only kind of artist for whom life drawing is a prime necessity is, it is obvious, he whose art consists in making drawings from the life. And this is a special line of business, though it is not often followed as a separate thing as it well might be. Drawing from the life, from the living model, whether naked or clothed, is seldom regarded as an end in itself. It is generally thought of as a means to other things—to the production of paintings or sculptures. This is a great pity. One can imagine no more attractive trade than that of supplying a willing public with good drawings of naked men and women. And the public is willing.

But artists, in spite of all the fuss they make about life study, very seldom take the thing really seriously as a substantive art—an art standing by its own merit. They call the things "studies," "sketches," "notes." They never really finish them and, in art schools, they are not even taught to *draw*. They are only taught to get somehow down on paper or canvas smudgy or scribbly imitations of the light and shade observable on the model. That a pencil or chalk or brush is a thing which of its nature makes a line if you pull it along is somehow forgotten. We are still taught to obsess ourselves with light and shade—to think of ourselves as a kind of camera. The thing called "line" and the shapes of things in themselves are seldom considered.

Now that a somewhat less puritanical and Manichæan view of life shows signs of emerging, it should be possible to make good drawings from the life and sell them just as picture post cards of Oxford colleges are sold or as they sell photographs of the animals at the Zoo.

And surely I cannot say more in favour of life drawing than this. I say such drawing is worth doing and it is worth doing for its own sake. It is not merely a means to other things—indeed, few other things need it at all.

But as all works of art are the product of the knowing and loving mind, so life drawing is. A good life drawing is not a photograph; though I have no sort of objection to photographs—they also have their interest and their use. A good life drawing, like any other work of art, is a translation into the terms of material—in this case, shall we say, the terms of paper and pencil—of the thing seen in the mind. And unless the thing seen in the mind be also known and loved the translation will be merely literal and such as a photograph could do better. That is why even the artist who draws from the life must also be a liver of life. Until you have lived you cannot know what is worth loving. Without the experience of life and that sort of sensibility which is necessary if experience is to be fruitful, a person's drawings will be merely empty reflections—worth nothing at all unless they be very skilful, and even if very skilful, worth nothing more than skill. Art is skill, skill is the very basis of art, the *sine qua non*. But it is the skill of men—not of ants or bees or mere mirrorscopes. It is the skill of men trained, disciplined by life, by the intellectual and moral *regimen* imposed by conscious life in society. Art is the skill of men employed in the making of things which they and their customers need and deem worth making. And life drawings are worth making and are needed just as portraits of our friends or of public persons are worth making and are needed.

But, except in the art of life drawing, drawing from the life is generally unnecessary and undesirable. It is often a seduction and a snare. It fills the mind with things irrelevant.

Suppose yourself asked to make a crucifix in stone. Would it not be ridiculous to hire a man to hang himself by the hands in order that you might discover how the muscles went and whether his arms came more or less out of their sockets? Clearly such considerations are quite irrelevant to the object. A crucifix is not a verisimilitude of the crucifixion. And even in a picture of the crucifixion the anatomical exactitudes are obviously a frivolity. What does it matter that no one has ever seen a living woman proportioned like the Venus in Botticelli's picture of her Rising? No one denies that the sculptures on the west door at Chartres are about as good as sculptures ever have been. Yet it is inconceivable that they did life drawing in art schools in the France of the twelfth century, and certainly there is no sign of such studies in their sculptures.

And, leaving ancient works out of it, to come down to common sense in fact, What's wrong with ordinary human life as a thing for providing opportunities for life study? If indeed we have forgotten the number of toes on our feet, what is to hinder us from a glance downwards or even a prolonged inspection, and much useful information can be obtained by looking in a mirror—even when the figure you are carving is that of a woman and you are a man. The members of your own household and your friends and relations are the best models. It's what you've got in your head that matters, and what you've got in your head has got to get there from life—not from textbooks and academies. Life is the means to knowledge, and you have to choose among the things you know to find the things you love, and it is from among the things you love that you must choose the things to carve—or to draw, or to paint. It is no use carving a thing just because you have learnt it in a book or seen it on a model—which is much the same thing.

For a sculptor, then, it seems that the living model is simply a kind of dictionary to which he turns when he is in difficulty about the spelling or accepted meaning. You do not go to a dictionary for ideas. The only artists for whom the dictionary, the living model, is a real and primary necessity is that special kind of artist whose job is to supply scenes from life. That kind of artist is, as I have said, a special kind. If he is more numerous to-day than at other times—so numerous as to make people think that his kind of art is art itself and art *par excellence*, the reasons for this are not difficult to find. They are many; but chief among them is the rise to supremacy in human affairs of the merchant man, the man of commerce.

It may seem that there is little connection between the ideas of business men and those of painters and sculptors. But in fact the connection is intimate and widespread and of paramount importance. He who pays calls the tune—in this as in other matters.

Another cause of the assumption that "scenes

from life" is the chief business of "artists" is the great break with tradition which we call "The Renaissance." At that time man discovered himself as *critic*. Painters especially, who had formerly been makers of furniture pictures—church reredoses, wall paintings of biblical or moral subjects, domestic decorations—became critics. They ceased to make things and became purveyors of pictures of things. That is to say, they ceased to make things for which the customer had *a need*, and for which the customer therefore *gave an order*, and they became makers of things "off their own bat," so to say, and depended on luck to find a customer who happened to like the sort of things they painted. And the things they painted, not being furniture ordered for this or that useful purpose, naturally became more and more mere expressions of the painter's own personality; they became essays in criticism—what so-and-so the painter felt or thought about things. Hence the rise to prominence of the great names. Henceforth the painter ceases to be anonymous, and his works are bought because they are *by him* rather than because they are *for his customer*.

And as the man of commerce became more and more the ruler, so the ordinary workman and supplier of furniture became more and more degraded.

To-day he is intellectually a nonentity; he is not expected to have a mind—at least he is not expected to have more mind than is necessary to enable him to do precisely, and without delay, what he is told.

On the other hand, as the ordinary workman became degraded, mentally deficient, and his work more and more dull, the painters and sculptors, musicians and poets, became more and more exalted, seated on pedestals, and their work more and more an expression of mentality alone, mentality isolated, isolated from all usefulness, and having no place but that of ornaments and museum pieces; and, if it may be said that industrialism has released the artist from the degradation of having to make anything useful, it must also be said that industrialism has released the workman from the exaltation of being anything of an artist. The workman has become simply a hand, a tool, a tooth on a wheel, and the artist has become simply a purveyor of sweetmeats—things curiously beautiful and entirely useless.

And what, under the circumstances, will seem sweet? What sort of things will our rulers, the men of business, be likely to appreciate? What, above all, will they pay for? And in such a world, a world in which the majority of ordinary workmen have been degraded to a subhuman condition of intellectual irresponsibility, the things which the master appreciates will eventually be appreciated by the men. What sort of things will be popular with the master? Remember we have a world in which, among the rulers (the men of commerce) and their employees (the factory hands) philosophy and religion count for nothing, count not at all. Philosophy has become the affair of dons (not that dons *have* philosophy, but they know all the differences between one philosophy and another) and religion has become simply ethics and ethics simply a code of police morality—not what is absolutely good or bad, right or wrong, true or false, but what is safe—"safety first" in a world of getting and spending. In such a world the most worshipful things are engines of power. Hence our worship of science and especially "applied" science—steam, electricity, chemicals. Hence, naturally, the cinema, the "wireless." Hence the photograph. Hence the worship of mere information, and hence of course the notion of art that it is no more than the business of "holding a mirror up to nature." Under the circumstances we need not find it surprising that those painters and sculptors and poets and musicians who do not regard themselves as mirrorscopes, whose works are not photographic, are not popular. Why on earth should they be? The trouble here is of quite a different kind. The trouble here is how to get employment without being parasites. How to get employment in a world which only wants photographs and no longer wants images; a world which no longer wants things of utility to be made by men for men—all such things are to be made by machines and in mass; a world which only wants works of art as a sort of extra, a gilding on the pill, a spare-time amusement, a thing having nothing to do with the really important business of living.

I dare say there is now no remedy and, anyway, the supply of remedies is not now my business. My business here is the statement of the fact that the work of the sculptor is the making of images and that images are things seen in the mind—the mind of man—man a creature who knows and loves. For such a workman the living model—flesh and blood—is simply one of the things we know, one of the things we love. We make an image of it in our minds—legs, bellies, stomachs, waists, breasts, necks, heads—heads, shoulders, backs, bottoms, calves, heels, feet, toes—toenails, navels, eyelids, ears, hair—all these things. Or if we prefer—hats, coats, cloaks, trousers, skirts, stockings, and boots. And all these things known, because lived with, and loved. If they be not known they cannot be loved, if not loved not worth making images out of. And all these numerous things are not only seen separately (though they may be so seen and must be so seen): they are seen in conjunction. They are seen together as parts which together make a whole. And every different image maker puts them together differently—makes a different kind of whole of them—because he has formed a different image out of them—thought about them differently—loved them either less or more.

In this connection I will quote the words of the German poet, Rainer Maria Rilke: "Verses," he says, "are not, as people imagine, simply feelings. . . . They are experiences. In order to write a single verse, one must see many cities and men and things; one must get to know animals and the flight of birds, and the gestures that the little flowers make when they open out in the morning. . . . There must be memories of many nights of love, each one unlike the others. . . . One must also have been besidc the dying, must have sat beside the dead. And still it is not yet enough to have memories. . . . Only when they have been turned to blood within us . . . only then can it happen that in a most rare hour the first word of a poem arises in their midst and goes forth from them."

So it is with all the arts.

So it is with the art of sculpture.

That is what the art of sculpture has been in the world since the beginning—it is the business of making materialisations of things formed in the mind.

But it is the business of supplying materialisations of things formed *in the mind of the customer* as much as of the sculptor. To sit on a pedestal and despise the customer is as abnormal as to grovel on the floor and worship the sculptor. And though we may doubt the wisdom of Bolshevik politics on other grounds we must at least admire it in this: that it is using artists, not to supply ornaments for the amusement of a cultured rich class, but to supply necessities for a whole people.

The great periods of art, that is to say of human work, have all been periods of great *communal* effort. Sculpture is the making of images of things known and loved. But to arrive at the highest possible grandeur they must be communally known and communally loved. Such a thing, as the late Professor Lethaby said, was mediæval architecture in Europe: "The work of a man a man may understand; but

[this] was the work of ages, of nations—nothing is individual or thrust forward as artistic; it is serene, masterly, non-personal, like a work of nature—indeed, it is such, it is a natural manifestation of the minds of men working under the impulse of a noble idea." Such a thing was Greek architecture and sculpture, such was Egyptian or Assyrian or Chinese. Such, pre-eminently, was Indian. And such indeed is modern engineering—of that also we may say: it is serene, masterly, non-personal, like a work of nature. And the noble idea which is its impulse is a thing in the minds of men. A work of engineering also is a materialisation of a thing formed in the mind, a thing known and loved.

I am making no claim therefore for art as "self-expression," as a means to the expression of individual idiosyncrasy. Every work of man necessarily bears the imprint of its maker. And it is good that it should be so; for man, alone among material creatures, knows and loves; and the imprint of such a creature, when he is free to make one, is delightful in itself, a sign of home, a greeting, as it were, from man to man. But man is more than men. Union is more than strength; it is depth and width and height also; and men fulfil one another. To strain after individuality and the expression of original views is

VII therefore to weaken rather than strengthen the work. To refuse the common knowledge and to eschew what is commonly loved and, instead, to dabble in curiosities and strange and exotic delights is to cut away the very root and stem of human art. On the other hand, no man can be commonplace on purpose and because he wishes to be as other men are.

There is no easy solution. You cannot by taking thought either add or take away a cubit from your stature or become either self-conscious or unself-conscious at will. Forget about it. Take up the work in hand. I know. I love.

VIII

ARCHITECTURE AND MACHINES

BY architecture we mean building considered as a fine art—that is to say, an art which subserves mental and not merely physical necessities.

Art is primarily simply skill—thus we rightly speak of the art of the dentist and of the pickpocket, and there is great art in washing up. Upon this lowly base is built up the grand erection of human accomplishment. To do or make something well is the root of the business.

But as it commonly happens that human works are used by human beings as well as done by human beings, it follows that the idea of suitability as well as that of utility occupies the mind of the workman. Hence even in the simplest articles of use the two ideas combine, coalesce or conflict, and the chairmaker who sets out to make simply a thing which will fit the sitting human body finds himself involved in all the complexity of the problems aroused by the question: what human body, or whose human body—am I making a child's chair or an office stool, a chair for the dining-room or one for the bishop in his cathedral?

Thus has grown up the distinction between art

and fine art. By art is meant simply the skill to do what needs doing or the skill to make what serves a physical use simply. By fine art is meant skill to do or to make that which is simply delightful to the mind. At the one extreme are such things as dentistry and pure engineering (though even dentists play about with gold stoppings for no real utilitarian reason), such things as working a London tube lift or mixing concrete for foundations, making horseshoes (nearly a lost art), or minding a telephone exchange —at the other extreme are such high things as Byzantine mosaics, the paintings of Picasso (which, whether you are delighted by them or not, are only intended for your delight), musical symphonies, poetry and dancing, and even sculptured stones.

But only rarely, if ever, do we get things pure. Only rarely are the works of men either purely utilitarian or purely delightful. Even the Forth Bridge is not purely utilitarian—the lower side of its great cantilevers are curved for no other reason than that its designer had the naïve idea that a curve was more pleasant to behold than a straight line, and, he remembered, all old and venerable bridges had arches, so the arch was the correct thing—the necessity of one age becomes the ornament of the next. And most things of use, when made by human beings, from kettles to cathedrals, are given by their makers an "ornamental" quality, if only because thus work becomes delightful to the worker. And by ornamental, of course, I do not mean simply added ornament or pattern business, but that quality in the form of things themselves which makes them delightful to look at, so that we are tempted to buy them, or steal them, merely to have them in the house, whether we have a "use" for them or not. And this delightfulness is not mere fancifulness; it is, as in the case of the chair, the quality by which things are suitable to rational minds, and not merely fitting for physical uses, even though the two things are not easily separable.

Most things whose primary purpose seems to be simple delightfulness and not usefulness at all, such as musical tunes or poems, have an element of physical usefulness. It is said that the poem originally was simply a sung accompaniment to work (as in the case of sea shanties), and much fine writing is simply the building in which useful information is housed.

Architecture is thus the type and mother of all the arts. Herein is combined, in equal balance and each in its highest degree, both what is useful and what is delightful. Architecture is not merely good building

VIII *—though good building is absolutely necessary to architecture.* Architecture is delightful building. It is building by which the mind of man is delighted.

But architecture, more than any other of the arts of man, is a social art. Even if it were possible for a single man, all by himself, to build a house, or even a garage, it would not be possible to build a house which he alone would see and use unless he were a hermit in a desert. Architecture more than any other art depends upon the collaboration of many men working and living together. What many combine to build many must necessarily see and live with.

It is not possible, therefore, to discuss the art of architecture as one might discuss the art of painting, or even the art of music. Architecture is not to be thought of in isolation. You cannot hang up a building on the wall of your bedroom or listen to it in the privacy of your boudoir. Nor can you say thus and thus I will build this building, as though you alone were going to do the work and you alone see it when done. You are forced, by the nature of the case, to take into consideration the facts that whatever you design will depend for its execution upon the labours of others, and that every building is a public monument.

And I am not urging this social view of architecture merely upon moral grounds. I am not simply saying that one should love one's fellow-men and not give them jobs they don't like to do or things that are offensive to them when done. I am not simply urging humanitarianism, nor am I endeavouring to inculcate a civic sense. Kindness to workmen or to one's fellow-citizens is right enough in its place, but it is not the business of architects *as such*.

The social nature of the art of architecture is important to architects primarily by reason of the fact that what is done by several or many men working in collaboration is necessarily different in kind from what is done by an individual working by himself, and what is necessarily used and enjoyed by many is different in kind from what is made for a private use. But the first consideration is the more immediately important here. Architecture needs an architect and it needs builders—design and execution.

And the first thing to notice about the building conditions of to-day is that, as far as the architect is concerned, builders are not men, but machines—they are not men while they are working, but only in their spare time—they are not artists (that is to say, responsible workmen), but hands, tools to be used by the designer, the architect, under whose direction they are guided, and whose word is absolute law. And not only so, but this condition is all they are capable of, and is indeed all that they demand. The builder is only too pleased to work according to the plans of the architect; the labourer or craftsman, whether trade unionist or not, is only too pleased to do whatever he is told.

I am not now going to bother myself as to whether this state of affairs is good or bad, or whether things have ever been different. The point is that this is the state of affairs *now*, and to act as if it were otherwise is simply foolishness. Let the social reformer do what he can about it; the architect's business is as much to make the best use of his "hands" as it is to make the best use of his materials. If his hands are fools, then his designs must be "fool-proof." If his materials are machine-made—the product of mass production and mechanised industry—then his designs must be of a kind that is suitable for such materials. In a word—we live in an Industrial world and, therefore, all ideas which derive from a time before Industrialism must be ruthlessly scrapped.

From certain points of view it is reasonable to hate this Industrialism. To a moralist it should be hateful because it is a tyranny; it was not voluntarily entered into by the workers; it was imposed upon them by grasping and avaricious merchants who had no aim but to make themselves rich. It is difficult to think of any introduction of machinery into already existing workshops which had any other object than that of lowering the costs of production and increasing the quantity of things made, and therefore the profits. No machine has ever been invented *for improving the quality*. Nothing has ever been done better by machinery than it has been or could be done by hand. Even now the best mathematical and astronomical and surgical instruments are hand-made, and the only things which can be said to be better done by machinery are things, like fountain-pens and typewriters, which could not otherwise be made at all except at a price which would make their use absurd, and indeed impossible except for those persons who don't really need them (see p. 184).

Also to a moralist Industrialism should be hateful because it degrades the workman to a sub-human condition of intellectual irresponsibility. Of no factory article can you say, "John made it—kick him"—or even "bless him." In a factory no onc is responsible for anything except for doing without delay what he is told.

To an "æsthete" also this Industrialism should be hateful, because it may seem to him that things made by the million lack that intimate personal quality which is proper to things made by men for men. He may look back to some pre-Industrial time as to a sort of paradise wherein all things made were works of art because all workmen were artists. He may think of the squalor and shapelessness of factory towns and the shrieking effrontery of commercial advertisement as things inseparable from Industrialism. He may think of the noise and mad hurry of the twentieth century, and he may

> *". . . dream of London, small, and white, and clean,*
> *The clear Thames bordered by its gardens green."*

But though, as a man, the architect may be a moralist, and, as a man, he may be an æsthete, nevertheless as an architect he is neither of those things. As an architect his business is the real business of building. And it is real building with real stone or wood or iron, and made by men as they really are—*just now*—and not as they were or as you would they were.

Architecture, I have said, is *delightful building.* What, under our present circumstances, can be really delightful? What can be the proper architecture of Industrialism? The Industrial magnate is primarily the avaricious man (except of course when he is making speeches about "honesty" and his duty as "a servant of the public"), and the Industrialist workman is an irresponsible machine-minder for whom there is no delight save what he can procure in his spare time—a man whose culture is not the product of his working life, but a compound of cheap sweets and highbrow welfare work—the cinema and evening lectures on the "wireless." What that is delightful can come out of a system in which the delight of the workman is absent, in which the delight of the workman is definitely ruled out as unnecessary and even undesirable? It is said in the Bible that "a man shall have joy in his labour and that this is his portion," but from the point of view of Industrialists this is simply "bilge water."

Up to the present the architects, soaked in past traditions and trained in museums of antiquities, have sought to obtain the necessary element of delightfulness (without which architecture is merely building) by what may be called the *veneering* method—that is to say, by the application of classical or mediæval façades and ornaments to buildings of which the true nature is nineteenth or twentieth century. Thus it has been considered proper that banks and town halls, even if they are built with a steel framework and brick partition walls, should have, at least in front, a classical composition of pillars and pediments, and that all details of doors or windows, door-knobs and fireplaces, should be moulded and ornamented with adaptations of classical mouldings and ornaments. Similarly, churches were thought to be properly in the Gothic style and private houses either Queen Anne or Elizabethan—a complete disregard of the progress of science or the real needs of men of commerce, and not only disregard, but even shame! Engineers were ashamed, and proud to be ashamed, of engineering. The engineer of the Tower Bridge, though the Tower Bridge is not a church, was proud to have his work completely covered over with imitation Gothic ornamental building.

But this veneering method of obtaining delightfulness is now approaching its end. With great pain and labour and in the face of much contumely and the opposition of snobbish interests and prejudices, a more honest, and that is the same as saying a more intelligent, method of dealing with the problem is coming to birth. Not a few architects, especially in France and Germany and Russia, have come to see that the same process as that by which the funny old "Rocket" evolved into such an excellent and good-looking thing as a modern locomotive could be allowed to take place in the business of building and furniture; that though architecture is concerned with what is suitable as well as with what is simply utilitarian, nevertheless the simply utilitarian is the proper basis for the development of the beautiful—that which is pleasing when seen. The labours of historians have dispelled the romantic clouds which had gathered round mediæval and classical remains. Gothic architecture is now seen to be primarily engineering in stone—a method of stone construction developed with strict regard to the necessities of the case, with hardly any eye to the picturesque effects it attained, with the word "beauty" hardly known, and never mentioned. Even Gothic sculpture is seen to be the product of "honesty and a strict attention to business." The sculptors did not talk about what art critics call "relations of masses," and confined their attention to the most vivid presentation of the subjects ordered of them by their customers.

But, for one reason and another, stone is no longer the material economically reasonable to-day. The size of buildings, the elaborate plumbing and lighting demanded, the provision of many floors, the necessity in modern towns of making buildings as fireproof as possible, in a word the countless conveniences required by modern standards, all combine to make it impossible to spend more than can be helped on walls and floors and roofs. Stone walls and groined roofs have gone, in fact, long ago. Only the outward skin of such things has remained, and now the skin in its turn, though it has hitherto seemed to be the chief reason for the existence of the architect, and is still the preoccupation of many old practitioners, is in its turn seen to be both unnecessary and ridiculous. The modern architect, if only to save himself from complete unemployment, is forced to be intelligent.

And the basis of intelligent building is "honesty and attention to business." Honesty: that is to say, facing the facts of men and materials and construction, and making the most of them. Attention to business: that is to say, proper consideration of the purpose for which the building is required, that it may be both useful and suitable.

Now under our Industrial conditions the most obvious fact is that men are mechanical and things are machine-made. To put into the design things which cannot be done by mechanics, or which cannot be properly made by machines, is simply silly. And all ornaments, even plain mouldings, are of this kind. Good modern building is plain—stark, staring plain.

Would any intelligent person have oak furniture in his dining-room which was covered, or even partly covered, with machine-stamped carving? Why, then, do comparatively intelligent architects think it right and proper to have the equivalent of machine-stamped carving on their town halls and churches? If your workman has been turned into a machine, then what he does with his hands is only "hand-made" in a sense entirely unimportant. Modern architectural carving is as much machine-made, and rightly so called, as anything done with an American carving machine. You can do good plain printing by machinery, but you obviously cannot do mediæval illuminated missals that way, and nobody now tries. But a lot of people still do not see that Corinthian capitals and Gothic traceries, "egg and dart" mouldings, and crockets and pinnacles, are just as impossible in an age of machinery. The old-fashioned architect, and of course his clients, think this outlook is gloomy. So it may be morally. So it may be economically. But it is not at all gloomy architecturally.

Good building, that is to say architecture, in an industrial age, is *plain* building. Plainness is a necessity. And plain means plain; it does not mean "comparatively plain," or "more or less plain." It means completely devoid of all carvings and mouldings. It means completely devoid of all those things which in any way spring from the exuberance or inventiveness of the man on the job. The man on the job is devoid of exuberance and inventiveness; it is no use designing his exuberance for him in the office.

But Plainness means more than merely devoid of all those things which spring from the exuberance of the man on the job; it means devoid of all those things which do not spring from the nature of the building as such—devoid of those things which do not spring from the nature of the building as a constructed thing or from the necessities of its nature as a thing to be used for such and such a special purpose.

Architects have during the last four hundred years regarded buildings entirely from the outside—both metaphorically and actually—and having designed the outside, they have then, more or less reluctantly or patronisingly and as a sort of concession to their clients, gone inside and contrived a few elegant "interiors." They have continued to do this long after all semblance of constructional necessity has departed from Gothic or Classic mannerisms.

But this is to view things entirely inside out. The primary necessity and origin of human building is the provision of habitations, of coverings, of roofs, of shelters—whatever word you like to use. Architecture is not to be thought of as a thing with a hollow space inside it, but as a covered space—a hollow space with a covering, and a covering naturally has an outside. The Greek temple and the mediæval cathedral both alike were designed from the inside outwards. The outside is the consequence of the inside, and owes its character and quality to the character and quality of the inside. A contrary view turns architecture into play-acting, the making of stage scenery; and stage scenery is the only name really applicable to most architecture since the Renaissance until quite recent times. From St. Paul's Cathedral to the new Regent Street Quadrant we have had nothing but stage effects obtained by viewing the job of building entirely from the outside.

The only architecture which is *properly* viewed thus is that of which some Indian temples and most cemetery mausoleums are examples. But these things are not really architecture so much as sculpture—they are not pies, they are a sort of blancmanges—they are not covered spaces, they are built-up shapes—they have no insides.

The root idea of building, and therefore of architecture, is the covering of a space, and the root of this idea is a physical need. These ideas have been submerged for four hundred years; they are now emerging again and forming a new architecture. And in this matter of mouldings and ornamentation these root ideas have their inevitable consequence. Cornices and pillars, pilasters and pediments, have obviously no place at all to-day because they spring from no necessity either of construction or suitability. And mouldings—what are they, after all, but a way of playing about with the edges of things? And playing about is just the one thing which is ruled out, because you cannot play about by proxy. Mouldings, however simple and however many miles there are of them, demand that the mason shall be, in however limited a degree, a responsible workman, an artist. The mediæval workman, the Greek workman, whether they were chattel slaves or serfs, were artists, however little they knew it, because they were responsible workmen. They were responsible workmen because in the absence of machinery and our highly organised methods of division and subdivision of labour; in the absence of paper on which to draw out full-size details of every stone they cut, *they had to be.*

But the thing that remains when all carving and ornament is omitted is, it comes to be seen, the thing with which the architect *as architect* is chiefly concerned—the plan and proportions and unity of the building—the thing which makes the building what it is. What sort of building *is* a bank? What sort *is* a church? What sort *is* an astronomer's telescope-house? Such different buildings are not distinguished by their carvings and ornaments. They are distinguished by the differences of their functions. Plainness, therefore, is not a hardship to the *architect*, even if other people find it depressing. The necessity of plainness is actually a release from the tyranny of things which of their nature are to-day both irrelevant and ridiculous.

Architectural sculpture, therefore, has no place in modern building. Sculpture, it is now abundantly clear, is not a thing you can exactly measure, and, therefore, it is not possible to make full-size details of it. If you do not make full-size details the trade-carver cannot proceed, and if you do not employ the trade-carver you must employ the studio artist, and that is ridiculous, because his work is of a different order of things from your machine-made building. The two goodnesses do not go together. It is like putting arts and crafts wrought-iron work on the Forth Bridge. It is like employing an illuminator to decorate your motor-car.

The only possible occasion for the sculptor on

good industrial architecture is the provision of heraldic signs; to distinguish the Church of St. James from that of St. Jude a statue on a corbel would be useful. To distinguish the building of the Prudential Insurance Company a statue of Prudence might be appropriate. Heraldry offers the only occasion for modern architectural sculpture. There are many such occasions. But for architectural sculpture, properly so-called, i.e. sculpture which is, as it were, the flowering of the actual walls of the building, there is now no occasion and no reasonable possibility. The enthusiasm of architects in the immediate future will find its proper field, therefore, in the development of plain building, and plain building, as has been shown by many recent experiments in that direction, gives scope not only for the greatest possible grandeur, but also for the erection of the only proper monument to the grand but inhuman genius of Industrialism.

IX
ART AND THE PEOPLE

(An address at the R.I.B.A. Conference, Manchester, 1932)

ART is in the first place skill, and, whatever other associations have come to attach to the word, skill is the necessary physical basis of art. But it is the skill of men—not of ants or elephants, and man is from his own point of view (whatever philosophers, or scientists with microscopes may say about it) a creature having free will—a creature responsible for his actions and responsible for the use he makes of his skill. Hence the thing called art is skill with human will behind it, and the object of the will, from man's point of view, and even from that of the scientist, the object of the will is the good. Hence the object of art is the use of skill in the making of good things. And this is the object of all the arts—from the lowest to the highest—from crossing-sweeping (a lost art?) to the painting of pictures and the writing of poems and symphonies.

Now powers develop with use—this is scientifically observable!—and conversely, they decay with disuse. A society which preserves among its people a strong sense of responsibility (for responsibility is the concomitant of free-will) and at the same time a clear notion of good (and a knowledge of good is bound up with a knowledge of truth; for you cannot will what is good without knowing what is good)—a society which preserves among its people a high level of responsibility and a clear notion of goods to be willed, will be a society in which the arts will develop strongly and it will be a society in which all ordinary workmen, as well as the more intellectually gifted ones will be, in a true sense of the word, artists—that is "responsible workmen." The people, in fact, will be "artistic"—history, both written and that which we preserve in museums, proves this conclusively.

On the other hand, a society which, under whatever influence of philosophic or religious or political change, fails to preserve full human responsibility among its members will be one in which the arts will languish among ordinary workmen and will become the accomplishment of specially gifted or rebellious individuals. Apart from the production of these extraordinary and eccentric persons, the only arts which will flourish will be the arts of engineering. Every kind of mechanism will be developed with enthusiasm and efficiency because such things are "patient," as the philosophers say, "of dialectical exposition." They are patient of measurement, they can be drawn on paper and expressed in figures;

above all, they can be ordered. You can tell a mechanic what to do and exactly how to do it. Nothing need be left to the workman except his obedience. The enormous and magnificent development of applied science which we witness to-day (and of which cities like Manchester are the product) is absolutely dependent upon the suppression in the ordinary workman of all intellectual responsibility. It has been said that "Industrialism has released the artist from the degradation of having to make any thing useful." I may say Industrialism has deprived the ordinary workman of the exaltation of being anything of an artist. And this result has been brought about first by the destruction of the peasantry and the small property owner—by the destruction of the power of economic resistance, and, second, by the development of machinery.

In the absence of machinery the slave, however economically bound, remains a responsible workman. He cannot do otherwise. (There is about two miles of Greek pottery in the British Museum—as beautiful as such work has ever been—it is all the work of slaves.) Slavery has existed in all periods of human history, but no slavery has been so absolute as that of our own time, because no previous slavery has been operative at the same time in both the economic and the intellectual spheres.

I said powers develop with use. And so it is with all human faculties. Eyesight, hearing, all the senses, are so developed. So also are the faculties of the mind—the intellect and the will. People who do not use their minds remain more or less idiotic. People who do not use their eyes and ears remain childish and half animal. Sensibility needs training as much as common sense. But training means doing things. You can't train yourself as a cricketer merely by paying a subscription to the club, or as a musician by listening to the "wireless," or as a painter by going to picture galleries, or as an engineer by receiving either a dividend or "the dole." You can't be an unskilled labourer by merely looking on. We are all trained by what we do, and no other way exists by which men may get either skill or cunning or culture.

But when we glibly join the words "art" and "the people" we are probably not meaning by the word "art" anything so commonplace or universal as mere human skill, and by the word "people" we mean anybody except artists. We take it for granted that artists are a special class; we regret their eccentricity and the immorality of which we have heard stories, but we do not regret—it does not occur to us to

regret—their specialisation. We either assemble as IX
benign "welfare workers"—moved by a desire to bring separated people into friendly relations—or, like some of our leaders of commerce, we desire to bring artists into touch with manufacturers simply in the interests of salesmanship. (I read in the paper only yesterday, that Sir —— had said, at another conference, that it was no use urging people to "Buy British" unless artists and manufacturers got together to make "British" synonymous with "artistic.")

But I take here another line altogether. Like most artists, I am a realist. I deal with real things and not more or less imaginary possibilities. I take it that we live in an industrial civilisation—and not in another kind. I know what an industrial civilisation is quite well. I am not under any illusion about it. Nor am I under the illusion that any but a very small minority of white men wants anything else. From the point of view of the great majority there's nothing whatever wrong with our civilisation but shortage of money. Very few persons are aware that the shortage is entirely due to the fact that the banks hold a monopoly for the issue of that convenience, but the majority are quite agreed that the shortage of money is the only evil in our otherwise admirable state of enlightenment. I say I am under no illusion about the nature of Industrialism. Industrialism means production for profit. It means a proletariat, i.e. a working class owning nothing but its labour power; it means the mechanisation of whatever can be mechanised and the mass production of whatever can be produced in mass. It means the specialisation of the arts of entertainment, whether the entertainers be professional cricketers and footballers or painters and poets. The West End picture gallery is just as much the show-place of professional entertainers as is the green grass at Old Trafford. Neither the working life of the rich nor that of the poor is a means to culture—both alike demand simply to be entertained in their spare time. The ideal of Industrialism is to produce short working time and high pay to spend on entertainment in a long leisure time. Industrialism means that whatever is deemed a necessary thing shall be made by machinery and in quantity, and only what is deemed unnecessary shall be allowed to remain in the sphere of those eccentrics called artists—eccentrics because in a world of slaves they choose to remain responsible for what they make. And those things only are allowed to escape the mesh of mass-production because, being deemed unnecessary, the demand for them is small, and there's "no money in them." Such is, in brief, the thing called Industrialism. We may regret it or we may not. That does not matter here. This is neither a religious nor a political meeting.

Architects, as much as sculptors, are artists, and therefore responsible workmen, and therefore realists. Architects, as much as sculptors, have got to work according to the conditions of their time. You can't build a Gothic or Classic cathedral to-day, even in Liverpool, without making a fool of yourself. It is said that function is insufficient for inspiration. It may or may not be so. The point is that no other inspiration is now available. All architecture which receives its inspiration in an industrial civilisation from any other source is pure play-acting, and the product is just stage scenery—the mere application of entertaining surfaces to things whose real nature is physical utility. Let such play-acting be confined to our places of entertainment—at Earl's Court or Blackpool. The people—the "people" go to the pictures to see the pictures, not to see the picture palace. And when it's not play-acting it's simply publicity—like a gin palace. The brighter the glare the less the other "pub" shows. So it is with the buildings of "big business"; they aim at imposing effects in order to "get away" with their impositions.

IX You can't impose on people without being imposing.

"Art and the people," then, means two things: it means, first, the art *of* the people—the art they actually produce; and, second, it means that which is produced for their entertainment or "uplift." As to the first: we know that under Industrialism the art of the people is the art of making things by machinery. That's what they do in their working time. Now what's to be said of machine-made goods? Just this: that they must be starkly plain—plain building to start with—no ornaments or sculptures, plain furniture and plain household utensils. Here's where the designer needs training, and first of all training in ordinary common intelligence. In Germany and Sweden they have got much farther in this than we have, and have shown that plain buildings and plain things are not only endurable, but much more endurable, i.e. when produced by machinery and in mass, than ornamental and ornamented buildings and things. The art of the people in an industrial civilisation should be plain art—the application of skill and obedience to the making of what is necessary in the way that machines necessitate and utility demands. But all bread and no jam is too dull—the people won't stand it. That brings us to the second thing, the art of Entertainment. To enjoy plain necessities demands a highbrow mind. The people are not highbrow—"the People," not only the working class but their employers as well. Therefore, as a set-off, the people must be entertained. But we must remember it must be entertainment suitable to people whose work demands nothing from them but skilful obedience and often obedience without skill—people whose work is no longer their means to culture—people whose tastes will necessarily be almost purely animal. And I mean "animal" in quite a good sense—healthy animal—football and games, including golf, lovemaking, and simple and sweet and rather noisy music with simple and exciting rhythms, plentiful and almost innocuous beer, cheap tours in charabancs. None of these things need be bad things. I'm not saying they need be anything but first-class in their kind. I am only saying that it is absurd to attempt to foist high æsthetics on people whose working life does not develop in them any intellectual responsibility. Nor am I saying that the things they produce in their working life, in the factory, or the things they deal with as clerks or shop hands, or transport workers, are or need be bad things. Plain things and plain buildings need not be anything but first-class.

IX Art is not just a few pictures in museums and picture galleries—any more than architecture is just the few buildings built by Fellows and Associates of the Royal Institute of British Architects. Art is *all* the things made in our time. Architecture is *all* the buildings. The Exchange Station in Manchester is as much art as the Royal Exchange in London, or the new *Daily Express* building. Sculpture is not only the works of a few well-known sculptors, but also the works of the church furniture shops.

But we are still making things and still building buildings according to the dregs of the fashions of pre-industrial times. We've got an industrial world, and we are proud of it (are we not?), and we have got industrial art—but it is nothing to be proud of. The thing to worry about is not whether the people get lectures on Shakespeare or conducted tours round the City Art Gallery; nor need we worry as to whether they have intelligent views on the merits of Gothic or Roman architecture. The thing to worry about is how to rid industrial art of its pretence to be anything but what it is. Industrial art must be plain—devoid of ornament. If people want ornaments they can make them themselves in that spare time they're so keen on (naturally factory hands and shop assistants don't want to stay in the factory or the shop after the whistle's blown or the blinds are down), or they can save up and buy the produce of the independent artist. It's not "the people" but the architects and manufacturers who need educating. They've got to learn that Corinthian columns and moulded stonework are as absurd on steel-framed buildings as arts and crafts wrought-iron work would be on the Forth Bridge. They've got to learn that hand-made ornament on machine-made furniture and pottery and household utensils is as absurd as inlaid mother-of-pearl would be on a motor-car bonnet. Moreover, it is unjust to the independent painters and carvers and metal workers to deprive them of their livelihood by supplying the people with necessarily bad machine-made imitations and reproductions. Above all, we must learn to leave out the word "art"—except as meaning simply skill —the skill to make well what needs making.

X
PLAIN ARCHITECTURE

(A letter to the Editor of "Architectural Design and Construction")

SIR,

In the paper which I read at the R.I.B.A. Conference at Manchester (see p. 141), I said that under the conditions prevailing to-day the ideas of architecture derived or hanging-over from pre-industrial times must be discarded, and that one inevitable result of the use of machinery and mass production, the factory system and the development of the division and subdivision of labour was the degradation of the majority of workmen to a condition of subhuman intellectual irresponsibility. I pointed out that the Conference was not convened to discuss social reform or the underlying questions of religion and that therefore any discussion of the goodness or otherwise of Industrialism was out of order. I pointed out, moreover, that the majority of people in industrial countries made no complaint except of the shortage of money; that far from there being any widespread desire to destroy Industrialism, most people were heartily agreed that twentieth-century civilisation presented an admirable spectacle of enlightenment. I said: we have got Industrialism, most people believe in it, few want anything different; let us see what kind of things are the best industrial products. X

Now, as I pointed out at Manchester, the main differences between our industrial civilisation and any that have preceded it are in the conditions of the workman and in the mechanical nature of his work. The industrial workman is not intellectually responsible (whatever he may think himself politically), and his work is not craftsmanship. He does not do merely what he is told to do; he does what the machine demands, i.e. he minds the machine in order that it may produce what it is designed to produce. Politically, he is allowed to wear the habiliments of a free citizen, but as a workman he is a slave and a slave of a kind that has not previously existed.

All this is sufficiently obvious. What is apparently not so obvious is the implications in the business of architecture. It is here that architects fall foul of me. They accept Industrialism; they do not see its consequences in architecture and the furniture of life. They think we can have a vital and widespread change in the conditions of workmen and in the nature of workmanship, and yet continue to behave and dress and build as though no change had occurred. And anyone who sees the change and its consequences and acts accordingly they suspect of charlatanry or perverse originality or of blindness to the value of tradition.

I quite understand the architects' difficulty in this matter. I was apprenticed as an architect myself, and have worked with and for architects for over thirty years. I know what an architect's office is like, and how fascinating is the study of ancient buildings. I know how comparatively easy it is to draw things on paper and how ready building contractors are to promise to execute whatever is drawn. You would like a focus point here or an emphasis there—put in some carving or mouldings. Do you like Tudor houses, and can you find a client who shares your predilection? Then what is to stop your having Tudor houses? The contractor won't refuse to contract; the workmen will not go on strike because you like Tudor houses and supply drawings from the smallest scale to full-size details. Or do you prefer "traditional English Gothic"? What does it matter that in every possible way we have discarded mediævalism in thought and in life? We can draw Gothic on paper, and there is no lack of workmen willing to do our bidding; i.e. faithfully and mechanically copy our drawings.

Tradition is a good word and a good thing; but X architecture is a social art. Buildings are conceived, but not built in the architect's office; nor are they built by the architect and his draughtsmen. They are the product of the whole society. For the smallest telephone call-box the whole resources of our civilisation are drawn upon. You cannot buy and shape a single plank of wood without the collaboration of thousands of your fellow-citizens. The growth of the

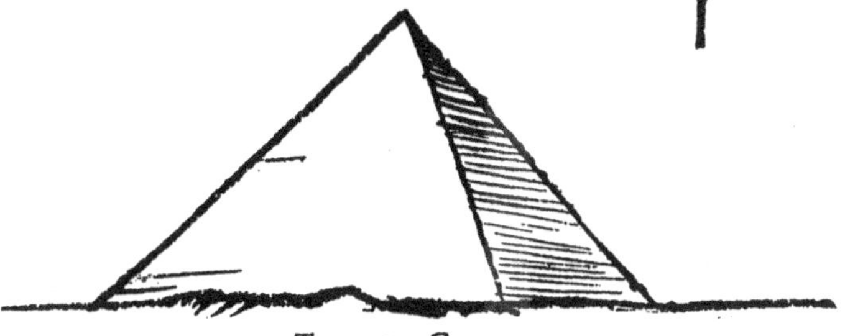

TOMB OF CHEOPS.

tree, the sawing, the transport, the tools required for these purposes and for the shaping of the wood in the workshop—none of these things is done or made without a nation's collaboration.

Office traditions, carried on by their own momentum, have led architects into by-ways and cul-de-sacs quite divergent from the main roads of our time. The thing architects call tradition is only the tradition of the architect's office reinforced by the snobbery and the prejudice of would-be cultured clients or clients who look upon architecture as a means to commercial or social aggrandisement.

And one of the traditions of the office is the notion, whether expressed in words or not, that architecture is chiefly the *outsides* of buildings. The engineer, civil or otherwise, can do the plan and all the construction, but you must call in an architect

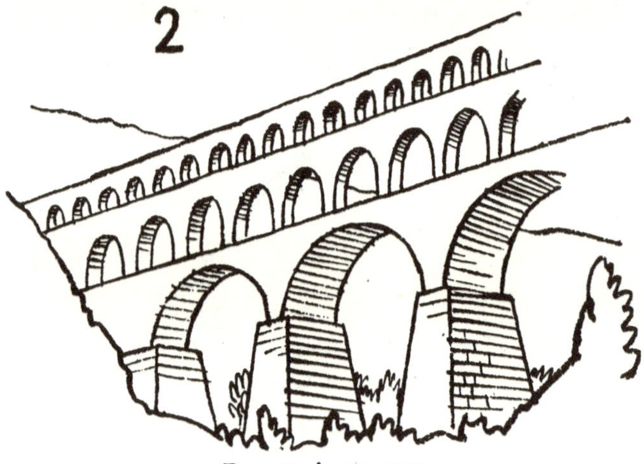

Roman Aqueduct.

to make the building presentable from the street. Ask an architect to draw you a church—a thousand to one and he'll see it in his mind's eye first of all as a contraption of towers and roofs and gables and buttresses. A thousand to one he won't see it first and chiefly as a canopy over an altar. And this concentration upon the outside effects of buildings leads architects to think of themselves chiefly as æstheticians and causes them to spin æsthetic theories to explain their position and maintain their prestige. They postulate an æsthetic sense which is not concerned with the purpose of a building (its "subject") or its construction. Hence the whole business of steel-framed buildings veneered to look like classical temples. And this æsthetic sense resides in the architect and his client; it has nothing to do with the building contractor and the men he calls his "hands." Hence the whole business of the nineteenth-century "Gothic revival." How could you revive mediæval architecture in an age of factories and machines except in the imaginations of architects living in offices and clients living in Walter Scott's novels?

However, let us suppose that all this is passing or past, that architects are coming or have come to agree that the subject-matter (the function of a building) and its construction (the method of its making) are of primary importance and the chief if not the only business of architects. Let us suppose that architects are agreed that if you look after goodness and truth, beauty will take care of itself—or herself. The beautiful is "that which being seen, pleases," and a thing which visibly fulfils its function and is visibly well-made is pleasing. To the artist, that is to say to the responsible workman, the subject is all in all. You cannot get a good house out of a man who does not heartily believe in the way people live in houses, any more than you can get a good carving of Venus out of a sculptor who doesn't love women. Supposing these things, I say, what sort of buildings shall we build to-day, in England, Industrial England? And if, among other things, I say that our buildings will and must be plain buildings, I am only saying what is in accordance with the conditions of building to-day. People say machines do not make anything, but that the phrase "machine-made" means "designed by human intellect and made by a man who chooses to use a machine in order to economise his labour." What a misunderstanding is here disclosed! Is the designer the same man as he who uses the machine? Does the man who uses the machine choose it? Is the machine user concerned to economise his labour? The factory system, Industrialism, is not like that. Industrialism means that one man designs the thing, another or several others design the machine to make it, innumerable nameless men use the machine because they are told to do so and their labour is economised by their employer because labour saved is equivalent to lower wages and bigger profits for him.

I am not here complaining about this. I am only saying that under the circumstances we are foolish if we go in for ornamental building. A plain wall is all right. Tons of concrete you can measure; millions of bricks you can count; thousands of "hands" you can

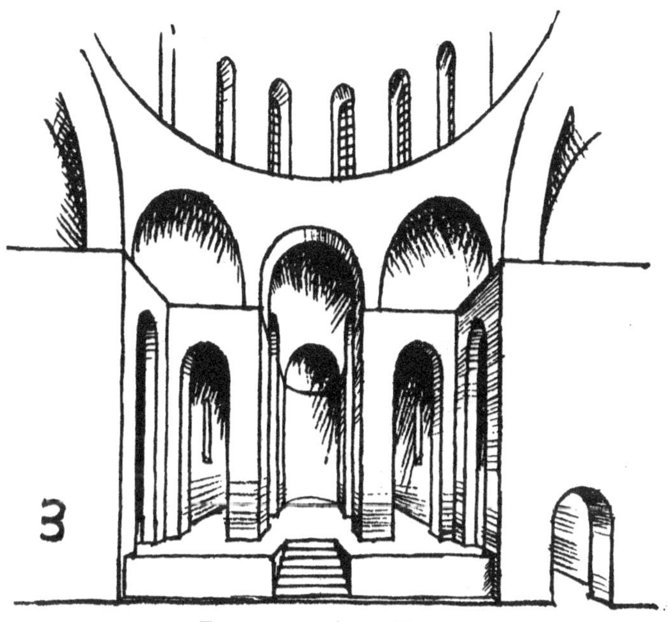

Church in Asia Minor.

command. But ornament cannot be made to measure and the best you can command is a lifeless copy of your full-size detail. There are still many architects and many more men of business who cannot see this. Nevertheless there are many architects who do see it, and it is they who are in a proper

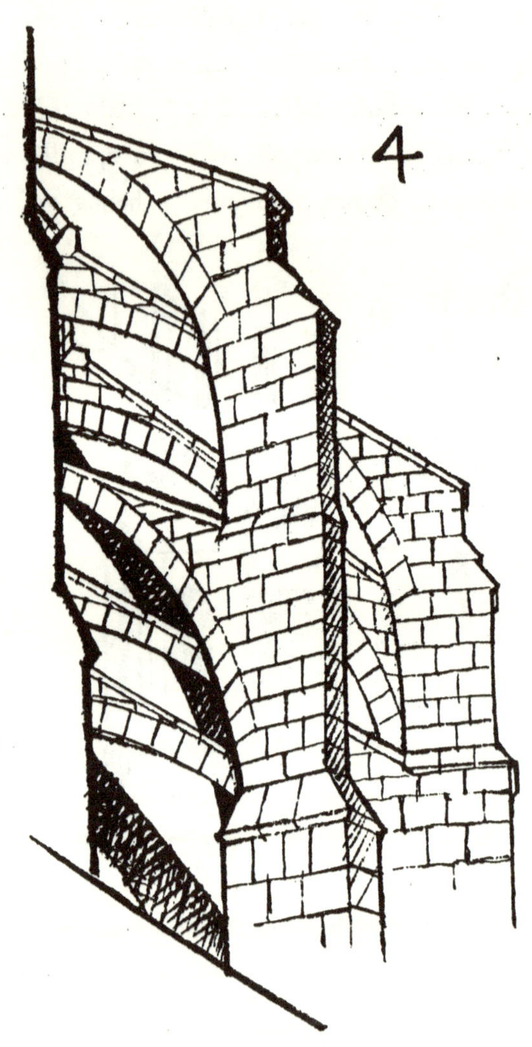

S. Pierre, Chartres: Buttresses.

sense modern. And as for the men of business, they can without any impropriety be told that what they save in carvings and mouldings and columns and pediments they can spend in grandeur of size and splendour of material. X

In your leading article, Sir, you express the view that it is strange or at least peculiar that I should "attach a special importance to the virtue of articles made by hand" and at the same time have a "sincere admiration" for things made by machinery. But, Sir, why should it be strange or peculiar that I should attach a special importance to such things as the sculptures of Chartres or of Mr. Epstein, the embroideries on the tunics of Russian peasants or Chinese mandarins, the penmanship of the Book of Kells or of eighteenth-century clerks (not to mention the letter-cutting of the Romans and of my own pupils), the bricklaying of the Elizabethans and the breadmaking of my baker, and at the same time sincerely admire a typewriter and a telescope, a skyscraper and an aeroplane, a motor-car and the ferro-concrete church at Le Raincy. I need hardly point out to you the special importance to be attached to human works. The whole trouble is as to the value of the human hand. Why not think of the hand simply as a tool? That being granted, we immediately see that it is a peculiarly sensitive and versatile tool. When the work to be done is of a kind which benefits by the use of such a tool, it seems silly not to use it. On the other hand, when speed and quantity of production appear to be of greater importance than sensitiveness of quality, then it would be foolish not to use machinery.

Our civilisation, having come to be under the rule of men of commerce and finance rather than that of princes or churchmen, has naturally come to consider speed and quantity to be of paramount importance, and in consequence a great stimulus has been given to the application of science to industry and to mechanical invention of all sorts. Concurrent with scientific advance has been the development of Industrialism; with the invention of machinery went the breeding of mechanics and factory hands. That such a civilisation means the degradation of the workman does not prevent it from producing admirable works. If no subhuman production could be admirable, then we should have to say that flowers, trees, animals were not admirable. Indeed, the sort of beauty that properly pertains to "machine-made" things is the same in kind as the beauty of what we call "nature." The beauty of a battleship or a good fountain-pen is the beauty of a beetle or a beehive. It is not my fault if this beauty is lacking in the radiance of human sensibility. We have elected to bring into existence the industrial state and that in itself means the loss of respect for men as fully responsible and intelligent beings (except of course in their spare time—what ho!), but we are not therefore debarred from admiring the ingenuity and power

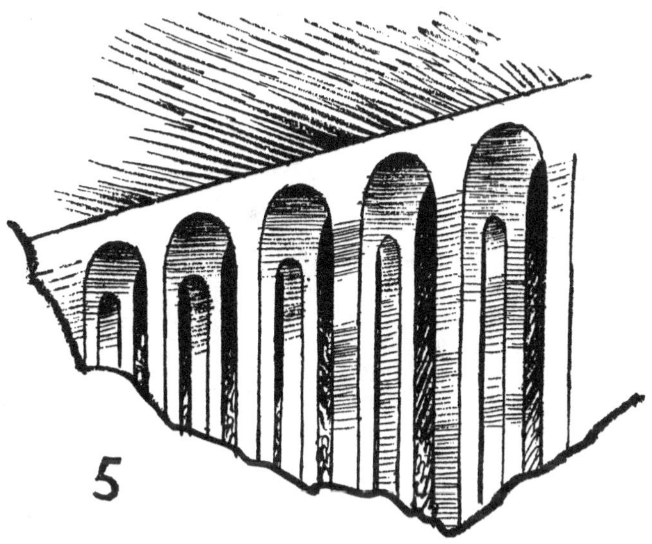

English Railway Viaduct.

which is visible in industrial products. All we are debarred from is the pretence that Industrialism is the same as Mediævalism, or that the industrial workman is capable of doing ornamental building.

I am challenged to produce "a drawing of the façade of any building that has the virtues which should characterise 'plain architecture.' " Of course

X I should be very pleased to comply, but the wealth of material is so great that I hardly know what to choose. Moreover, most of your readers can have no difficulty on this point, and I shall be merely point-

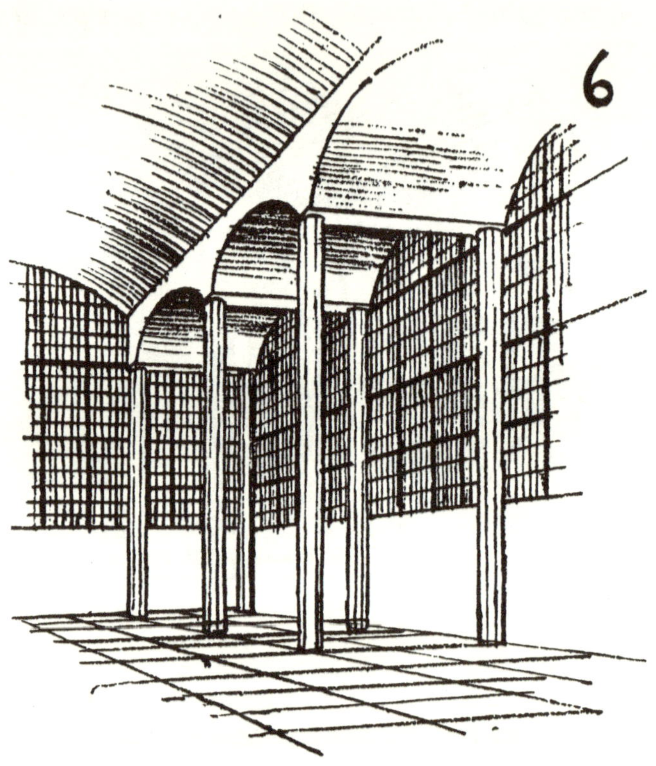

Church near Paris.

ing out what is obvious to them. Plainness is a negative virtue; it is a privation, an asceticism. All that I contended to the conference at Manchester was that architects should, under industrial conditions, curb their natural exuberance as draughtsmen—leave out the frills and fal-lals and burn the glossaries of ornament. Nevertheless, plain building has been done in all ages—even in the most boisterously unindustrial times—so there is no need for me to be so impudent as to play the architect and invent a building *in vacuo.* I append, therefore, a few diagrams more in politeness than as necessary to my argument.

P.S.—Some people are keen on "Nature" as a textbook for artists. It should be noted, however, that the apparently ornamental features of flowers and animals are not added by conscious artistry from outside. They are a development depending upon the functions and requirements of the creatures. Let the ornament of industrial buildings so develop. See my diagram, No. 4. The flying buttress may be regarded as an ornamental feature, but that is not its *raison d'être.* Art imitates Nature "by working as she works"—not by imitating her appearance.

XI

PAINTING AND THE PUBLIC

(A speech at the opening of a picture exhibition at a restaurant)

MY immortal fellow-guest[1] once said that it was "funnier to have a nose than to have a Roman nose." There are many things like that. For example: it is funnier to be a Catholic than a Roman Catholic—that is to say, it is funnier that a man should have *any* religion than that he should have the true one. Again, it is much funnier to wear trousers than to wear Bond Street trousers, and when I sit eating my lunch in a Lyons teashop it becomes abundantly clear that it is much funnier to eat anything at all than it is to eat even the Lyons "portion."

But, thinking of this meeting, perhaps the funniest thing of all funny things is the thing called art. It is funnier that there should be *art* than that there should be any particular kind of art, however fantastic.

And this is specially true in these days. The word art of course means first of all simply skill—human skill. Thus we have the art of the dentist and that of the pickpocket, and thus we have the word "artful," which is much the same as "crafty." But there is a

[1] Mr. G. K. Chesterton.

special sense of the word art which we are concerned with here, and in this sense art is not mere skill, though it involves skill (for nothing can be done or made without at least a little skill). Art in the sense we are concerned with is the thing made rather than the skill in making—and further, it means the thing made delightfully rather than the thing made skilfully—the thing made for the delight of the person who sees it (or hears it, or touches it, or tastes it, or smells it) rather than made simply for the convenience of him who uses it. It is work raised above the plane of physical utility to the plane of intelligent pleasure or delight; to the plane of the beautiful (the beautiful thing is that which being seen pleases)—the beautiful more or less consciously willed by the workman and consciously sought by his customer.

But until the era of Industrialism (the approach of whose full development—it is not yet quite complete—we are now witnessing) the work of utility was commonly the occasion of the work of beauty, the delightful work, the work of "Art." The line of demarcation between workman and artist was not between the picture painters (sculptors, musicians, and poets) on the one hand and, on the other, the people who made all the other things. There was no hard line of division. Every object of utility was in some degree a work of art.

This was necessarily so and without any self-conscious or "high-brow" fuss about it—in spite of war, pestilence and famine, battle, murder, and sudden death; in spite of chattel slavery and serfdom; in spite of the tyranny of princes and the avarice of men of business—because, in the absence of a highly developed system of divided and subdivided labour, in the absence of elaborate machinery, in the absence of cheap drawing paper and therefore of measured drawings supplied by architects and engineers, every workman was in some degree a *responsible* workman—responsible not merely for doing what he was told but for the quality, the intellectual quality of what his deeds effected. He was a more or less independent person who was expected to use, and was paid to use, his intelligence and, therefore (if only to make his work pleasant in the doing—for, as it says in the book of Ecclesiasticus, "a man shall have joy in his labour; and this is his portion"), he was a person who did to some extent, either more or less, regard the thing to be made as a thing to be made delightful as well as useful.

But we have undoubtedly changed all that—not quite, but very nearly completely—and when I say "no ordinary workman is or could be an artist," no one will say I am lying; on the contrary, everyone will say: "of course not."

The ordinary workman it is who by mass organisation makes the ordinary necessaries of life and even many of the luxuries; and whether or no it be necessary that *luxuries* be produced in mass, it is now clearly unnecessary that *necessities* should be produced one by one by independent individual artists.

The professor of fine arts in the University of Edinburgh has put the matter in a very small nutshell. He has said that Industrialism has released the artist from the necessity of having to make anything useful. All ordinary things are made for ordinary people by ordinary people working in factories. Artists are those special people who make special things for special people. Artists are the only responsible people left—because they are the only people who are really responsible for what they make—the only people you can still blame if what they make is bad. And as they are less and less called upon to make useful things (i.e. things physically useful), they are more and more sought after on account of their personal gifts of temper and sensibility. Hence the great insistence upon the artist's individuality, upon his personality. Hence the notion

XI that art is self-expression—the expression of the artist's self. As emotion, feeling, sensibility, cannot be shown in machine-made things, it is thought that art exists specially for the expression of those things. As Clive Bell put it: what matters about a picture is not what you *think* about it but what it makes you *feel*. I don't say he's right, but that's what he said. And so art, divorced from the common life in which men make useful things (whether hats or hammers, houses or ham-sandwiches) becomes a more and more fantastic or at least eccentric extra.

Now artists live by selling what they make, and those who buy very naturally buy only what they like (what "appeals" to them as they say). And because there is every sort of buyer there is every sort of artist—from the purveyor of the sweetest chocolate-box pictures of creamy English beauty to the most fantastic kind of all—namely, that which makes it appeal *exclusively* to the person of disinterested intelligence and sensibility.

But if the artist wants to live more or less in the same way as his contemporaries (according to the same standard of living), wear the same kind of clothes, have baths as the best people in Wimbledon do, eat similar food and dwell in houses such as will pass the building regulations, then he must, he simply *must* make things which his contemporaries like, even if he makes things which they can only like for the wrong reasons.

Making things which people like for the wrong reasons is, indeed, the first trick to be acquired by the artist unless he be content either to live as a hermit in a desert or to depend for his livelihood upon the favour of a special coterie of wealthy æsthetes.

What is commonly thought and often said about the artist's function is mostly nonsense—that it is his business to teach, to lead, to guide the world out of its natural and muddy ditch into the cultivated fields. This pedestal or pulpit upon or in which the artist has been placed is an erection of very recent, almost contemporary, design. The artist as prophet and seer and teacher is the creation of very modern times—times which are once again witnessing the submergence of all interests beneath commercial interests.

But the kindly and very sentimental man of business is frightened, and no wonder! at the consequences and accompaniments of his rule. And, as everyone wants to have his pudding and eat it as well, we have the spectacle of Mr. Henry Tate building the Tate Gallery, Mr. Carnegie founding libraries, and all sorts of lesser men going in for "a spot of culture" in their spare time. But we do not witness any attempt on their part to destroy the commercial system itself—the system of usury which we politely call Capitalism and the system of slavery which we politely call Industrialism. I doubt if there are more than half a dozen people even here who wish to destroy either of those things.

Nevertheless everybody is agreed that there are some things which they cannot produce in factories, which can never be produced in factories, very desirable things—at least things which very many people desire, things the very nature of which is that they are the product of responsible workmen, workmen working as human beings for human beings and not as irresponsible tools for the benefit of an impersonal thing called "the common good." Paintings and engravings are among such things. They cannot be produced by the factory system.

It is not primarily a question of machinery; it is not that painting could not be done with the aid of a gas engine. It is primarily a question of the responsible workman. For the production of a painting you must have a responsible painter—someone whose will it is that the paint shall be put on just here and not just there. The very *essence*, the great *charm* of the factory is that you do *not* need workmen who want to impose their free wills, their idiosyncrasies, their emotions and sensibilities upon the design and manufacture of razor blades.

I say the great "charm"—for it makes the business so much simpler from the point of view of management and, ever since Adam said "Eve did it," shirking responsibility has been the chief temptation of ordinary men and women.

It is true that the Medici Society can have a factory for the reproduction of existing paintings—thus making painters even rarer birds than before; but though artists become rarer and rarer they can never be replaced, because there must be originals before there can be reproductions.

However, do not let us be deceived by this rosy picture. The artist, as such, is irreplaceable; but the public, the thing which pays the money, is quite content with substitutes. If the walls of the Lyons teashop are covered with marble and the wireless is "on," the public is quite happy, and there is simply nothing in its daily life and work to develop any capacity for knowing a good painting from a bad one.

A painting consists of two things: its subject-matter and its paint. You may, if you like, forget about

XI the paint, or if you prefer, you can forget about the subject. If the former line be your enthusiasm, if you are not interested in the possibilities of paint as paint, you can go to an art school and gain the skill necessary to make your painting look so like the life of flesh and blood, that from a short distance away, people will not know that it is made of paint at all. If your subjects are "popular" ones, you will be a "popular" painter. (But what sort of subjects are likely to be popular with men of business and factory hands?)

If, on the other hand, your enthusiasm leads you in the other direction—that is, if you are so intelligent as to recognise that the popular subject business has gone to pot, if you are too intelligent to take upon yourself the business of prophet and seer in addition to that of painter, and yet not intelligent enough to become "as a little child" and have your subjects given to you by "authority"—then you can devote yourself to pure æsthetics and problems of the studio and make your "appeal" to the few æsthetes who have money enough as well as the will to support you. It is remarkable how many there are of them; but it still remains funnier that there should be *any* people who like art than that there should be many people who like *fine* art.

I should like to add by way of postscript that nothing I have said implies any denial that motor-cars and fountain-pens, telephones and aeroplanes and iron girders and typewriters and electric light and wireless and type-setting machines and all the other gadgets profitably exploited by men of commerce (for of course they never invented anything themselves) are all clever things and wonderful things—everybody agrees that machinery is marvellous, "jolly fine," splendid, and even beautiful to look at.

Nor does anything I have said imply that all the paintings of the twentieth century, and the sculptures, music, and poetry, are mere charlatanry or even mere essays in practical æsthetics. I do not wish to mention names, but I think there is no doubt that the work of modern artists has carried the business of the expression of human sensibility, the sensibility of human beings to the spiritual implications of their physical environment, very much farther than it was carried by most artists of earlier periods, artists who, by the condition of their times and by their traditions, were more concerned with what is called "literary content" (or as I should say "subject-matter") and with the service, even the physical service, of their customers than the modern artist is. "What I ask of a painting," said Maurice Denis, "is that it shall look like paint," and I might say: "What I ask of a stone-carving is that it shall look like stone." Modern artists have, very rightly and in spite of the Royal Academy, at least set themselves to explore their materials. They have in fact rediscovered their materials. They have rediscovered the fact that a painting or a sculpture has a value for what it is as well as, and independently of, its value as producing an illusion of being something else. They have rediscovered the fact that the artist's business is to make *things*, rather than to produce *effects*.

As to "subject-matter," that is properly the customer's business; in the first place, because the customer only orders what he *wants;* and, in the second, because he only buys what he likes—in the second case it is simply as though the painter had anticipated the customer's order. If you paint something with the idea of selling it, you are, in effect, doing the same as a manufacturer who makes Christmas cards six months before Christmas. And from the point of view of the customer it is, with the rarest possible exceptions, always the subject-matter which is the important thing. When you show him a picture he asks, "What is it?"—unless, of course, he can see at a glance . . . and the exceptions are only apparent, for even in a picture which has no subject-matter or literary content in the ordinary sense, there is still a subject even if it can only be described in such terms as: "the visual relations between a top-hat, a banana, and a glass door." Such a subject may appeal only to the few—it is none the less a subject, and it remains true that it is for the *subject* that the customer normally puts down his money.

It should be added, by way of warning to both buyers of pictures and those who merely look at them, that the subject of a picture is not merely what it is stated to be in the catalogue or in verbal descriptions.

Catalogue titles are often only "catch" names to distinguish one picture from another, and when a customer says: paint me a "Madonna," or a picture of "the Derby," or of some "roses in a bowl," the painter must know, and *this is the crux of the matter*, what precisely those words mean in the mind of the customer. The word "Madonna" may mean no more than a simpering maiden in the conventional attitude of the church-furniture shop. A picture of the Derby may mean anything from a photograph of the winner to a representation of the whole universe. A painted bowl of roses may mean only a naturalistic painting of roses such that I, who live in a flat, can think I have a bit of garden on my sitting-room wall, and very pleasant too!, or it may mean the concentrated essence of all the roses God ever made, or it may mean that the roses are only a *spring-board* from which the mind has jumped and the painting is the consequent *splash*. It may mean almost anything else also. But, whatever it means, the artist must know or guess. Heaven help him!

The trouble to-day is *not* that the artists do not take any interest in subject-matter. The trouble is that the mind of to-day is, roughly speaking (and not very roughly), the *Daily Mail* mind. The trouble is that so few customers can put forward a subject worthy of an intelligent artist's attention.

Nevertheless, in spite of the great quantity of fine works produced by the reaction against the banality of the Academy subject-picture, the pure æsthetic line of business is, in the nature of things, a cul-de-sac—a blind alley at the end of which is a sort of hot-house for the cultivation of man-eating orchids.

The divorce of art from common life, the divorce of the artist from the company of ordinary workmen, the absence of any subject-matter exciting enough, even interesting enough to command and control their enthusiasm, and the consequence that artists are thrown back upon pure sensibility or else pure charlatanism—such is the state of affairs. I am not a politician that I should suggest remedies. I can only hope that under the benign influence of good food and good drink people will continue to buy the works of those who, in spite of everything, are the only responsible workmen left.

I apologise for the extremely elementary nature of my remarks. I confess I like elementary lectures much better than the advanced kind. As Mr. Belloc used to say during the war: "Two come from the left, and two come from the right—making four in all."

XII

ART AND INDUSTRIALISM

Art——

What's the good of it?

"What's it all bloomin' well for?" as the young giant said in H. G. Wells's novel.

Is it "generally necessary to Salvation"? as the C. of E. Catechism puts it.

¶ ART is skill.

Man's art is deliberate skill—skill used deliberately—with deliberation—i.e. of one's own free will.

I.e. as the result of choice—choosing to do this rather than that.

For that is what man is—a creature having "free will" —i.e. power of deliberation and choice.

At least men *think* they have free will, and act accordingly and judge one another accordingly.

(The philosophical question can be left out of this discussion—whether we really have free will or no, we all assume that we have, and artists especially assume that they have power of choice.)

Art is deliberate skill used for the good of something to be made,

Not for the good of the maker,

Nor for the good of the buyer,

But for the good of *the thing itself.* XII

¶ There is another use of the word "art," i.e. when we use it, not as the name of the thing made—the *work* of art—but when we mean the act of the *mind*, the act of making in the imagination, when we say: "Art is a virtue of the practical intelligence"—the intelligence not merely apprehending ideas or things, but actually *imagining* things—making things in the mind.

I assume that this sense of the word art underlies all that may be said of *works* of art.

Works of art are the product in material (space-time) of what has first been conceived and made in the mind, in the imagination.

Nevertheless, the *word* art means

First of all *skill*.

Skill in *making* (ΠΟΙΗΣΙΣ).

¶ Art is concerned with making things.

Art is only concerned with deeds in so far as they relate to the thing to be made.

The deed in itself is not important.

But, with man, all doing tends to become making, to become *art* work, all things become works of art:

E.g. Hitting with hammers. Who has not watched blacksmiths or navvies at work? Navvies in circle. And who cares what is being hit? The hitting has become a thing, a thing made—like a dance—an art, a thing pleasing in itself, worth doing for its own sake—a game, and like all games, essentially an art.

¶ The artist is the man who makes things, that is his function. He does things—but only in order that something may be made; that it shall conform to the idea of it which is in his mind, the idea or image.

First, he must get the idea of the thing to be made clearly in his mind. He must know and *see* precisely *what it is* that he would make.

Secondly, he must desire to make it. If he is to make it well he must see it clearly in his mind, and he must desire it strongly.

There must be no half heart about it.

Clear knowledge and strong desire.

Thirdly, he must have skill—at least sufficient skill.

But this skill depends upon knowledge and will.

It is no use being skilful if you do not know, if you cannot *imagine* what you are making.

It is no use being skilful if you have no desire, no will to make it.

But, also, it is no use knowing and willing if you have no skill in doing. XII

It is skill in doing that gives us the name artist—i.e. skilful man (artificer, artisan, artful, and hence we speak of the art of the dentist and the art of flying, etc.).

When we speak of artist the knowledge of things and the desire to make them is taken for granted in him.

Many besides artists have knowledge of things.

Many besides artists desire things.

The artist is the man with sufficient skill to *make* them.

¶ All men who make things are artists.

Until the Industrial Revolution there was no need to talk about it.

Formerly, before James Watt produced the first efficient steam engine, whatever had to be made there was someone, some *man*, who made it.

From ships to sealing-wax, from shoes to sculptures, everything was not only man-designed, it was man-made.

Not only were all things works of art, i.e. the works of men employing deliberate skill, but all workmen were artists—more or less.

XII I.e. responsible workmen, workmen responsible for the good or bad quality of what their deeds effected.

This is not so to-day—

nor will it be so to-morrow.

To-day artists are peculiar people.

(Hot-house plants—comic turns.)

The majority of things made to-day are not made by men at all.

The majority of men to-day do not make things.

They only do things.

They only do what they are told.

They are not responsible for the thing which results from their obedience.

They are not responsible workmen.

They are not artists. They are puppets.

They have been reduced (as the theologian puts it) to a subhuman condition of intellectual irresponsibility.

They are more interested in the process than in the product.

¶ Most things to-day are made by machinery.

That is to say, they are made as the designer of the machine or the manager of the factory intends, and not according to the design of the user of the machine—the machine minder.

Tools have been used by men since the time of Adam. XII

Machinery, in the usual sense of the word, has only been used since the time of James Watt.

Tools are labour-*saving* devices.

Machines are labour-*displacing* devices.

Tools help the workman.

Machinery makes the workman less necessary and, eventually, unnecessary altogether.

The object of tools is to improve the work done.

The object of machinery is to lower the costs of production.

Tools may be called machines and vice versa, but "machine made" can't be called "hand made."

¶ It takes, it is said, eighteen men to make a pin.

Not one of them can be blamed if it have no point.

A thousand men combine to make an ocean "liner."

Not one of them can tell his girl he is a ship-builder.

A thousand "hands" combine to put up a modern building.

Not one of them can claim responsibility.

Yes, there is one, there is the architect—the designer. He is the only artist, the only responsible workman.

XII This is not a question of good or bad. It is simply an explanation of the fact that the artist is a peculiar person.

It is the same in all trades:

Building: the architect alone is to be praised or blamed.

Furniture: who makes what Mr. Drage sends out on hire? Is even Mr. Drage responsible?

Clothes: can any ordinary person who buys ready-made clothes blame anybody if they do not fit?

Utensils and tools: if your fountain-pen will not write, or your "lighter" won't light, or your knife will not cut, what can you do but take it back to the shop?

¶ But, yes, in every department of life there are a few artists, a few responsible workmen left, a few peculiar people.

Among builders, to a thousand hands there is one architect.

Among furniture makers, there are a few independent carpenters.

Among clothiers, there are still a few "West End" tailors.

There are a few dressmakers, a few independent weavers and dyers, a few knife grinders—and of course there are lots of people with hobbies

—people who do what they like *in their spare time.* XII

¶ But of all the independents the most notably and notoriously independent are the painters of pictures and the sculptors of images—also writers of books and poems, and those who make music.

It is these people who are to-day almost exclusively called artists—their independence and responsibility is so obvious. (Though, of course, the man of business likes to talk about irresponsible artists—he calls them irresponsible because they are responsible to themselves and to their own customers and to society at large and not to *him*. *Liber est causa sui, servus autem ordinatur ad alium.*[1] The freeman is responsible for himself, for the slave another is responsible.)

The artist is the responsible workman. Because he is responsible for his work his reputation is at stake, and if he makes things badly he will be out of work—he will starve.

The artist's business is to make things *well*.

All well-made things are beautiful.

It is only the accident of our time that the only

[1] St. Thomas Aquinas, *Summ. Theol.* IA, Q. 96, Art 4.

workmen who can be held responsible for the quality of what they make are picture painters, sculptors, writers, and musicians.

These people are artists, not because their work is beautiful, but because they are responsible for it.

A factory hand is not responsible, therefore he is not an artist.

His master is not concerned with making things well; he is only concerned with making things that will sell.

Hence the association of beauty with the work of those other workmen who have escaped the slavery of the factory.

Because the free workman is concerned for his reputation as a *good* workman and the good work is the beautiful work.

¶ The beautiful thing, what is it but that which being seen pleases? *Id quod visum placet.*

The beautiful thing is a thing visible and knowable as an object.

It is not simply something reasoned about.

It is not something regarded merely as a means to an end.

It is a thing seen and regarded as an end—in itself, an object.

And it is a thing pleasing, primarily to the mind, the mind which knows and wills.

The more the intelligence is fogged, the more the will is corrupted, so much the more dubious the pleasure.

A bad painting is one whose painter has not known clearly what he was painting—has not seen it clear in his imagination or who has not known the nature of paint—has not seen the thing as a *painting*. ("What I ask of a painting," said Maurice Denis, "is that it shall look like paint.")

Or the painter's will may fail him—he may not have cared enough about it.

Or, given both knowledge and will, mere dexterity may be wanting.

But dexterity is generally sufficient when knowledge and will are adequate.

And people who are pleased with bad paintings are like bad painters.

They are ill-informed as to the nature of the thing.

Or their wills may fail them, as when a person says: "I know it's silly, but I can't help liking it."

And, even if it seem difficult to believe, it is true that paintings and sculptures and poems and music are governed by the same laws and reasons as govern buildings and furniture and sewing-machines and hammers and hats.

You must first know what a thing *is* before you can judge it.

Suppose someone asks, What *is* a good picture?

One might as well ask: What is a good colour? or, What is a good shape?

The only possible answer to such questions is on the purely physical plane. On that plane one might reply: A good picture, a good colour, a good shape is simply one that does not *hurt*.

When we say: The Apollo of Tenea is a good sculpture, we mean, first, that it is a good sculpture of *Apollo*. The knowledge that it is a certain kind of ideal young man is taken for granted—and taken for granted as being necessary.

A monkey wouldn't know that it was good.

A little girl of three years old wouldn't know that it was good.

Secondly, when we say that the Apollo of Tenea is good sculpture we mean it is Apollo as he ought to be in *stone*.

The knowledge that it is not flesh and blood is taken for granted.

It is taken for granted that the thing is a thing of the imagination—that it owes its being to the imagination, that it was a thing seen in the mind of the maker and a thing seen by its maker *as a thing of stone.*

It owes its being to the marriage of matter and spirit.

Man is matter and spirit—both real and both good.

Apollo is a creature of the mind—a spiritual being.

The Apollo of Tenea is matter as well as spirit—stone and mind wedded—one flesh.

Every *work* of art is made of these two—matter and mind (or spirit).

The ordinary man who refuses to judge a thing until he knows what it is, is quite right.

He asks: What is it? and if he can't see at a glance you must be able to answer him.

Talk about good sculpture, good painting, good form, good colour is mere studio talk, studio jargon, except with reference to what the thing is.

Only when we know what a thing is can we go on to consider the studio business.

The Tenean Apollo—is it Apollo, and if so, is it as he ought to be in stone?

Buckingham Palace—it is a king's house. Is it built as a king's house ought to be built?

The inscription on a coin. What is lettering? And is it lettering as it ought to be on a coin?

XII The Martyr's memorial at Oxford—what are martyrs ? and is imitation Gothic their proper memorial?

A dining-room chair—what is dining—who are the diners? Is the chair suitable to such a place and occasion and suitable to those who dine—men and women, not cats and dogs.

A book—a printed book. What is a book, what is printing? A thing to read. What thing? and what is the act of reading? Good printing is not only what is harmless to the eyes, but also what is delightful to the mind—the mind of man—man a creature who knows and loves—not merely an animal, a mechanism which lives and dies.

Church music—what is a church? What is music, and is it made as it ought to be for a church?

Music may exist simply in the mind of the musician, but, even before he puts it on paper, it exists in terms of musical instruments.

Moreover, it exists in terms of the place and occasion of its execution.

A concert hall is as much a place as a church.

A concert audience is a group of human beings as much as a church congregation.

You cannot sing to nobody nowhere any more than

you can make horseshoes without reference to horses and roads.

When a person says: "I don't know anything about art, but I know what I like," he is making a perfectly just remark.

What he likes: that is to say, what pleases him.

We only ask, just as we demand it of artists, that he take some trouble to exercise his mind—his apparatus for liking—that he keep his mind in good training.

"A good life is a mortified life."

Good taste is mortified taste.

Mortified—that is, taste in which the stupid, the sentimental, the irrelevant is *killed*.

Art is the making of things.

To-day the word art is used only of what are called the "fine" arts—those arts which aim specifically and consciously at the making of things of beauty.

Because in all other arts the responsible workman has been done away with.

Industrialism has released *the workman* from the necessity of being anything of an artist.

And Industrialism has released *the artist* from the necessity of making anything useful.

XII The factory article claims to be useful, and really useful things are always beautiful, but beauty is not the conscious aim of the factory hand.

The work of art claims to be beautiful, and beautiful things are often useful, but usefulness is not the conscious aim of the artist.

So we have separated the idea of usefulness from the idea of beautifulness.

Because we have separated the idea of work from the idea of responsibility.

¶ We still ask Messrs. Maple to supply us with beautiful chairs and tables, but Mr. Maple cannot allow any individual workman to make a complete chair or table and be responsible for it.

The designing of Maple's furniture is done in a drawing office.

The draughtsmen are not responsible even for designing.

They, being in need of money, are paid to draw what Mr. Maple's experience shows him is most saleable.

Competition to obtain the buyer's favour is not between furniture designers as to which can design the best furniture, but between salesmen as to which can most successfully tickle the fancy of buyers who have no standards by which to judge the quality of anything.

They are at the mercy of lying advertisements and the lure of snobbery.

So it is in all trades.

It is the price we pay for cheapness and quantity.

Many of the conveniences and furnishings of modern life simply could not *be* if we went back to the old methods of manufacture in small workshops by independent and responsible workmen.

Fountain-pens and motor-cars, etc., can only be brought within the means of ordinary people by standardised production and divided and subdivided labour.

¶ Art is the making of things.

Fountain-pens and motor-cars are as much works of art as pictures and sculptures.

The only difference is that fountain-pens and motor-cars and such things are not the product of one or more rcsponsible workmen working on their own responsibility and dealing more or less directly and personally with their known customers—they are the product of many hands working under obedience.

XII Instead of many artists, that is, responsible workmen, each making what he deems good, we have one designer—one artist—one responsible workman—and a host of willing or unwilling "hands"—willing if they be well paid and decently treated, unwilling if pay be short, hours long, or amusements few.

That is why strikes are common in industrialised societies.

Having no interest in their work—how can you have interest in your work if nothing you do or say affects it one way or another? Men are driven back upon purely moral considerations—conditions and hours of labour, equalities and inequalities in the distribution of wages, considerations bearing upon anything but the work itself.

On the other hand, employers and their managers and directors, apart from the few artists (responsible designers and inventors), generally have equally little interest in the work itself provided it pays, that is, provided it sells.

Capital and Labour under industrial conditions are necessarily two opposed parties.

Capital pays the lowest wages consistent with

efficiency and organises things, so that whenever possible time and labour and material and costs are saved.

Labour does as little work as is consistent with keeping the job—though conscientiousness in the workman has less and less to do with keeping the job.

Machinery throws more men out of employment than any lack of conscientiousness in the workman.

To the employer the work is the thing which brings in the profits.

To the employee it is the thing which brings in the wages.

Neither has any reason to care what the work is.

Labour is as fluid as capital.

Both can be transferred from one trade to another without either capitalist or labourer noticing any difference.

Such is Industrialism, and its blessings to the consumer are numerous and remarkable.

We are all consumers, even if we are not all labourers or capitalists.

Countless public and domestic conveniences are now obtainable which kings could not formerly enjoy.

XII ¶ Art is the making of things.

A motor-car is a thing made.

Therefore a motor-car is a work of art.

Its designer is an artist.

The men who make it are not men. (They have been reduced to a subhuman condition of intellectual irresponsibility.) They are "hands."

They are the hands of the designer.

The only difference between the artist who designs, and by means of his factory "hands" makes motor-cars, and the artist who designs, and with his own hands paints pictures, is that the motor-car designer is more strictly and consciously concerned with the physical utility of the thing to be made than the painter is.

The beauty of a motor-car is the product of its functional suitability. The beautiful thing is that which being seen pleases—we are pleased by the sight of good machinery and good machine-made things because we are able to recognise in them their admirable economy.

Their beauty is like that of bones and beetles and trees and flowers and the bodies of animals and human beings.

The beauty of paintings and such things is also the product of functional suitability.

But the function of such things is not primarily a physical suitability. It is primarily a *mental* suitability.

¶ The motor-car designer is an artist.

The innumerable men and women who are employed in its manufacture are not artists.

They are not responsible workmen.

This is of no consequence as far as the motor-car is concerned.

On the contrary, it will be disastrous to the motor-car manufacturer if he cannot rely upon an adequate supply of obedient "hands."

I.e. until he can obtain machines to replace them.

It must be remembered:

The object of an Employer is not to provide employment, but to produce goods at a profit.

He is only an employer of labour *per accidens.* He has no *desire* to employ labour.

And the Employer has not even any desire to produce *goods.*

His desire is to enjoy life and power.

He employs labour to produce goods.

He produces goods to obtain "profit."

He desires "profit" in order that he may buy enjoyments.

And most of the things he buys for his enjoyment are produced in a similar frame of mind by other employers.

Whether among Capitalists or among Communists (whether the speaker is Mr. Selfridge or Mr. Lenin), the dope is the idea of "service," the service of humanity, the service of one's fellows.

But note: this is purely dope.

And it is a purely moral dope.

It is simply a matter of good will.

Good intelligence, good sense, sensibility in the workman is not asked for.

Temperament in a factory hand is a nuisance—both to himself and his master.

Such things would be out of place.

Such things are relegated to spare time—the time when you are not at work.

The time which those who have dividends call "Leisure."

We already live in the "Brave New World."

¶ Whether we like it or not, we are breeding, we have already bred, a puppet population which has not only lost all sense of responsibility for the work it does, but no longer desires to regain such responsibility.

The intellectual standard has in consequence become exceedingly low. XII

Consider the kind of things everybody likes and buys.

Consider the furniture Mr. Drage lends.

Consider the songs which are most popular—the pictures and ornaments.

These things are turned out merely to tickle the fancy of an entirely uncritical people—a people inevitably uncritical because it has no use for criticism—it is never under the necessity of being critical except in matters of purely physical convenience.

The result of Industrialism has been, not merely to concentrate wealth, and therefore power in the *hands* of the few, thus making the bulk of the population a wage-earning proletariat—that is comparatively unimportant from this point of view (if everyone is happy . . .), but it is to concentrate intellectual responsibility in the *minds* of the few, and to make the bulk of the population an intellectually irresponsible herd—depending for its food, shelter, clothing, and amusement, for its books and opinions upon what the few wealthy big business people find it profitable to supply to them.

XII We may note that "big business" finds it profitable to supply inferior goods rather than superior, trash for books and lies for news.

Meanwhile the individual artist becomes more and more the "hot-house plant" depending for his support upon the small class of cultured connoisseurs whom art critics and dealers can persuade to invest their money in his works.

This is inevitable, for the work of the independent responsible workman must more and more reflect his increasing eccentricity—his increasing isolation—his now almost complete divorce from the normal business of producing what is useful and necessary to ordinary men and women.

Moreover, even when he calls himself an artist craftsman and makes what are supposed to be utilities, his work is out of keeping with its surroundings.

It belongs to another world—"a world that has had its day."

Hand-made sculptures *look* absurd and *are* absurd on machine-made buildings.

Hand-made furniture *looks* absurd and *is* absurd in machine-made houses.

Hand-made clothes *look* absurd and *are* absurd in

motor-cars and omnibuses and on the backs of machine operators.

Hand-made jewellery *looks* absurd and *is* absurd on machine-made gowns and shirt fronts.

The place for hand-made things is the museum.

The dearest ambition of painters and sculptors is in consequence to have their works bought for the museums called art galleries.

The hand-printed book is kept in the museum called the glass case.

Industrialism (how often must it be repeated before its implications are understood?)—Industrialism has released the artist from the necessity of making anything useful.

Industrialism has released the workman from the necessity of being anything of an artist.

Labour-saving gadgets have made culture a spare-time product—"the B.B.C. of science" is supplemented by the B.B.C. of culture.

Throughout human history culture has been the product of the work men did for their livings.

Henceforth it will be the product of a special Government Department—the Ministry of Leisure.

¶ Moreover, labour-saving gadgets, it seems, really have saved labour.

XII There are, it is said, some twenty to thirty millions of people to-day whose labour is unnecessary.

And as machinery is being improved hour by hour, both in ingenuity and in power, there will undoubtedly be fifty millions for whose labour there is no need before many months have passed and then a hundred millions.

It is only a banking difficulty which makes the present "dole" so inadequate.

There is no reason why the "dole" shouldn't be thought of and called a "dividend."

There is no reason why we should not have a world in which everyone has plenty of food, clothes, shelter, and B.B.C.-ish amusement, and also plenty of spare time—and, curiously enough, and sad as it may seem to those who profit by the sale of that particular kind of "labour"-saving gadget, also plenty of babies.

¶ All this depends, *first*, upon our ability to depose the bankers.

They are living in a *pre*-industrial world. Their system of accountancy is out of date.

Secondly, it depends upon our willingness not merely to forgo our responsibility as workmen (for we shall *all* have to become factory hands for a few hours a day, or, at least, a few hours a week), but also and equally important, our willingness to eat standardised food (as most people do already), to wear standardised clothes (as most people also already do), to live in standardised houses of absolutely plain kind with plain standardised furniture and utensils (for standardised ornament is very quickly nauseating) and be entertained by standardised entertainment (unless we are the sort of eccentric individuals who can actually entertain ourselves).

That is to say, that the business of farming and food producing, the business of weaving and dressmaking and tailoring, the whole business of building and furnishing, the three main businesses of human life, the businesses which have hitherto been man's chief means to the production of things for his delight—eating, dressing up, and building—will be cut out of the sphere of art work, and will be relegated to the sphere of the drains—mere utilities, mere necessities, necessary evils.

¶ And these standardised things won't necessarily be bad things, and therefore not ugly things or unpleasant things. Lots of people like "Grapenuts." Most people prefer factory bread to home-made. Germany and Sweden have shown us how excellent standardised furniture and utensils can be. Plain standardised buildings are already very good, and much better than Victorian Gothic, or Edwardian sham Roman. A good standardised rational dress could easily be better than our present silly fashions of tailor-made upholstery.

In your spare time you can do what you like. You can keep sheep and grow wool and weave your own clothes (provided, of course, that you do your share of the work of the standardised clothes factory as well).

You can, I suppose, do fretwork or water-colour painting—for your local museum.

You can, I don't see what's to stop you, even build a house for yourself alongside of the standard house for which you will pay rent and tax.

You can have your private kitchen garden and eat your own cabbages. But surprisingly few will grow food for a hobby.

¶ And you must not say you don't like this scheme of life.

It is quite inevitable, because *no one wants to abolish machinery* and the banking system must inevitably be altered—it is already discredited.

The only alternative is the complete collapse of our civilisation, and nobody wants that. XII

But perhaps that is what will really happen.

Perhaps collapse is the inevitable end of a civilisation which has allowed labour-saving tools to be replaced by labour-displacing machinery —a civilisation wherein men, in thrall to financiers and men of business, have surrendered their responsibility as workmen.

XIII

BEAUTY LOOKS AFTER HERSELF

Religion is the affirmation of values—both relative and absolute.

Philosophy is the statement of causes—both physical and metaphysical.

Men can only deny one another's conclusions when they accept one another's axioms.

THE unity of the human race must be taken for granted. Differences between one person and another or between one race and another and between the people of one time and another are simply differences of emphasis. This being so, it is to be expected that all human beings and all races will look to the same end, and all differences of achievement are to be attributed not so much to differences of aim as to differences of temper and circumstance. These facts are the more important when the subject of discussion is, as in the case of the arts, a thing of which the achievement has been so various and, as in the case of religion and philosophy, a thing of which the expression has been so apparently contradictory, and when, in addition, the subject is complicated by racial and geographical differences.

Now the end of the human race, the end to which all activity is directed, is the discovery and grasping of the real. However variously this end may be described or pursued; however erroneous may be the conclusions of reason; however distasteful may be the material achievements of one people to a people of another time or place; nevertheless Reality, what is real and not illusory, is what is sought by each and by all.

It may be said that "the real" is an object of interest only to philosophers, and that I am wrong in saying that ordinary people are concerned with the search for it. It may be said that *happiness* is what all men seek, or the *good*, or the *true*, or the *beautiful*. It may be said that what all men desire, aim at, work for, is simply physical security and well-being—safety and a full stomach.

But although these various things—happiness, the good, safety, repletion are often stated to be men's aims, it will be found, I think, on analysis and inquiry that these various things all come to the same thing—viz. *reality*. Only in what is real can men be happy; the unreal cannot be the true; what is not true cannot be good; the radiance of reality turns out to be the only beauty; safety is valueless except as a means to enjoyment and, ultimately, reality is alone enjoyable. Finally, to eat in order that we may work in order that we may eat in order that we may work in order that we may eat is a circle from which even the lowest men seek escape.

Now either we may accept as real only what is immediately apparent to our senses or, at the other extreme, confronted by the countless evidences of the invalidity of conclusions drawn from immediate sensory experience, we may accept as real only those things of which we have immediate interior knowledge. At the one end is the ordinary, unthinking and, as he is called in Western society, "practical" man (though it may be doubted whether a perfect specimen of him really exists), at the other are they who hold that mind alone is real and that "the universe only exists for him who perceives it." In between is every sort of mixture and compromise. The typical materialist of Western commercial civilisation is confused by the dregs of other traditions; moreover, he takes even his religion of science for the most part on the authority of journalists and popular writers, and very little or not at all on the evidence of his own senses or as the product of his own reasoning. The idealist, on the other hand, is constantly aware of circumstances which, even to himself, seem to demand at least a temporary or conditional assent to the notion of material reality. Urgencies of appetite and of physical pain mar or destroy his detachment, and as, in the beginning, "Adam sinned when he fell from contemplation," so men of all times and places have, whether willingly or unwillingly, surrendered at least for a time to sensuality and the things of sense.

But while the materialist compromises with spiritual things, and the idealist compromises with material things, and some men refuse any compromise whatever, it remains clear that all men are concerned to discover the real. The materialist's denial of the reality of spirit is an affirmation of his belief in the reality of matter, and the idealist's denial of the reality of material things, except as ideas in his own mind, is at least an affirmation of his belief in the reality of his ideas. We are all realists in this sense: that we all believe something is real, and the world consists of three classes of men: those who believe in the reality of matter and the validity of sensory experience and who deny the reality of spirit; those who believe in the reality of spirit and deny the reality of matter; and those who believe matter and spirit are both real—that both have real existence and that matter is not an illusion imposed upon purely spiritual beings or spirit an illusion suffered by beings who have no existence except such as is measurable in terms of time and space.

XIII By real existence we mean existence independent of the perceiver—for example: that God exists whether I perceive Him or not; that the world of things exists whether I perceive it or not. On the other hand, it must be remembered that it cannot be said that the world of things exists independently of God's perception of it unless the existence of God be denied. Also it is well to point out that a belief in the reality of matter need not imply a denial of the παντα ῥέι of Heraclitus or Mr. H. G. Wells or an acceptance of Nietzsche's declaration that "there is no being behind doing . . ." and that "being is a fictitious addition to doing." We may admit the perpetual "flux," and we may at the same time affirm the reality of that which "flows."

We are all realists; we are all moved by enthusiasm to discover and embrace what is real. And however lacking in philosophical exactitude their statement of the case may be, all men desire to live and act in accordance with the truth, and all men abhor the notion that there is no truth anywhere discoverable. We are all realists; but according to our notions of reality so will our works differ. Could there be a world of men in which God, pure Being, were universally believed to be the only reality, such a world of men would, without doubt, produce a different civilisation from that produced by a world of men, could there be such, who universally believed the evidences of the senses to be the only valid evidence, material things the only real things, and matter a perpetual becoming, a flux of measurable motion. I am not here saying that either world would be right or wrong; I am simply saying that different forms of life, different shapes of things would result according as one or the other notion of the truth were paramount. Nor am I here saying that the things resulting would in either case be better or worse; I am simply saying that they would be different, and that the notion that men are automatons whose acts and works do not reflect their minds is as unthinkable as it is historically without foundation.

And if a completely atheist civilisation, could such exist, would inevitably produce different works from a civilisation completely God-fearing, so every civilisation produces works reflecting the bent of its intellectual enthusiasm. The spiritual enthusiasm of mediæval Europe, no less than that of more ancient and more modern India, was reflected in its works, its temples, and its laws. If many churches were built it was undoubtedly because many churches were wanted. So great an expenditure of time and treasure could not conceivably have been made upon things considered unimportant. Whatever we may think of their religion or philosophy, we cannot imagine that they would have done or made the same things if they had had different ideas about man's place and destiny. The fact that to-day in England we spend more time and treasure erecting buildings for the conduct of commerce and less in erecting churches does not prove that we have neither religion nor philosophy, but simply that our religion and philosophy are different. We seek reality as much as at any time, but we hold it to reside more certainly in material things, in measurable things, in things for which the senses are evidence, than in spiritual things, immeasurable things, things which cannot be proved by experiment. The buildings of commercial England are just as much evidence of a state of mind as are the buildings of mediæval Europe or India.

And what applies to buildings applies equally to all other things made by men. If we seem to give our attention here chiefly to the sphere of painting and sculpture, music and poetry, it is not because we deny the influence of religion and philosophy in other spheres, but simply because in this sphere the human state of mind is more evident. In such works the human being is more obviously a mentality at work; in such works mentality more obviously predominates, is ruler. In other works, as for example in the making of bicycles or sewing-machines, mentality plays a less conspicuous part. Such machines are little more than the contrivances an ingenious animal might evolve. The bicycle is no more ingenious than the web of a spider or the hive of a bee, and is only more intelligent because it is consciously contrived. In such works man is chiefly moved by the needs of his animal nature. Such are for the most part the things, the works, for which we have in modern Europe and America most enthusiasm. This does not show that we have no religion or philosophy, but simply that we hold no end to be so excellent or so attainable as material success and, as many of our writers bear witness, we worship matter with the same emotion that, in other times and places, is aroused by the worship of God. Or, shall we say, for us God is power and impersonal, but formerly they said God is Love and a person.

"The Divine beauty is the cause of all being," said Denis (the Areopagite or another) and St. Thomas Aquinas. And East and West, ancient and modern are all agreed about this. But the modern West, following Nietzsche, says "when Power becometh

XIII gracious and steppeth down into visibleness—Beauty I call such stepping down" (i.e. that Beauty is incarnate *power*). Hence the huge development of Industrialism in nineteenth-century Europe and America. On the other hand, the ancient West and the East, both ancient and modern, hold that beauty is incarnate *Love*.

We hold, then, that every person and every people is concerned to lay hold of reality, and that all the works of men display this concern. We hold that different peoples and different times display different works because among such peoples and in such times different notions of reality have been accepted.

Now the phrase "notion of reality" is simply another way of saying Religion and Philosophy. To say, therefore, that the works of men reflect and are the product of their "notions of reality" is the same as saying that the works of men reflect and are the product of their Religion and Philosophy. Religion and Philosophy are as necessary to the production of such monuments as the Forth Bridge or the Aqueduct at Nîmes as they are to the production of such monuments as the Cathedral of Chartres, the Pyramids of Egypt, or the Temples of Ajanta.

But it is not possible to have both kinds of things.

You cannot serve two Gods at the same time. You can have a civilisation of which the main stream of production is works of material power. Such is the civilisation of twentieth-century Europe and America, and its most complete development will be found in Soviet Russia, where the doctrine that the works of men reflect and are the product of religion and philosophy will be very clearly exemplified. The essence of religion is the affirmation of absolute values. In Russia the absolute value of the community is affirmed. The worship of man in the communal collective sense is the religion of Russia. Italy, Germany, France, England, and the United States of America—each in its own way is developing the same ideas. In all these countries the subordination of the individual and the family to the group or herd is now about to become absolute. In all these countries the value of material power is receiving absolute affirmation. The philosophy of materialism is the preamble to this religion of power. The human soul and its immortality is more and more commonly doubted. When it is at last completely denied, what will be left but the determination to gain the whole world? Let us eat, drink, and be merry, for to-morrow we die.

The gigantic development of Industrialism (the

factory system and mass production) in Russia shows that the Russian Communists are not inspired by the desire for a different *kind* of world from that desired by Capitalists in other countries. The difference is simply in the distribution of the product. The capitalist civilisations desire that the profit of Industrialism shall remain with or go into the hands of the owners of capital, while self-interest, becoming, as their own phrase puts it, more "enlightened," endeavours to curb proletarian discontent by a wider distribution of benefits (higher wages, shorter hours of labour, the provision of entertainments, etc.). The Russian Communists, pushing Marxian Socialism, as they aver, to its logical end, desire that the only Capitalist shall be the community in its collective capacity, and that the distribution of benefits shall not depend upon the "enlightened self-interest" of a class, but shall be the inevitable and universal reward of a just distribution of human suffering.

Both Capitalists and Communists desire the destruction of private enterprise; i.e. they both detest the small farmer and the small craftsman and the small shopkeeper who, like doctors, lawyers, and other "professional" men, attempt to support themselves in independence of "big business" or State enterprise. Such persons are the natural enemies of either the Capitalist or Communist State. They do not "serve." Their notion of service is not that of Mr. Selfridge or Mr. Lenin. Such persons tend to believe that the world is better served when independent but not isolated workmen produce what each considers his best than when masses of workmen, controlled and directed by appointed overseers, produce the largest possible quantity of things which no individual considers holy and no one considers even good or beautiful except in the sense that whatever is truly useful is to that extent good and, like bones and battleships, beautiful.

On the other hand, you can have a civilisation which, whether statedly or not, produces as its primary and most obvious product works of love, and only secondarily and incidentally and in a primitive, amateurish kind of way, works of convenience and works of power—e.g. a primitive sort of sanitation, transport by animal power, handlooms, and tools such as workmen make for themselves. Such have been the civilisations of all peoples not ruled by men of commerce, of all civilisations informed by a philosophy and religion in which the absolute value of the spiritual is affirmed.

Good men, that is to say men of courage, tenderness, generosity, are common in both kinds of civilisation and in any compromise between the two. It is no part of my contention here that all materialists are wicked. Nor am I here concerned to say whether a philosophy of materialism contains more or less of truth than one in which the reality of the spiritual is affirmed. It is not here a question of good or bad, of true or false. The whole point here is that whatever men do or make, their philosophy and religion are at the back of it, and that those who deny this are compelled in consequence to admit that the works of men are either the product of purely animal instinct (that the Forth Bridge and the Venus of Milo are no more than a sort of beaver's dams) or that they are the product of simple caprice.

I am not saying that the works of men, Hindu, Christian, or Atheist, are good, because there is this or that philosophy and religion behind them. I am saying more than that. I am saying that it is because there is this or that philosophy and religion behind them that they are there at all—that it is to this or that philosophy and religion that such works owe their very existence, their very being.

Doubtless there are many actions that men do and even many things that men make, which may plausibly be claimed to be the simple product of animal instinct; for man is a kind of animal, even if he is also a kind of spirit. His appetites for food and shelter continue to operate even when his destiny as child of God and inheritor of the Kingdom of Heaven is forgotten or denied. He will fly from physical danger even when he will not pursue spiritual safety. He will endeavour to crush what hurts him—as a snake in the grass—even when he will not bestir himself to make things for his delight. Let those who will develop our knowledge of the animal side of men's doings. The psychologists, from McDougall to Freud, may be trusted to leave no avenue unexplored. Everything that can be said for man as animal will be said sooner or later by them. There is no need for anything to be said here.

We take here the ground that, whether or no first in time or place, the most important motives for man's activity in doing or making are neither animal instincts nor caprice. We hold that mind, including both sense and sensibility, is more important and not merely more dignified than instinct. Upon such a ground and from such a place of vantage we survey the works of men. We see all things as evidence of mind. We make what we *believe* to be good—in accordance with our beliefs so we make. A pair of scissors, no less than a cathedral or a symphony, is evidence of what we hold good and therefore worth making, and owes its being to mind.

The materialist philosopher of our day sees all things in terms of physical force; for him mathematical laws are the ultimate laws, and he seeks to bring into his "mesh system" both mind and matter and to explain them mathematically. Those, on the other hand, who from the beginning saw all things in terms of the spiritual mind, saw all things, even mathematics, in terms of love, and they seek to recapture from the materialist wider and wider and deeper and deeper spheres. I say recapture, for they do but regain what formerly they had. This great system of materialist philosophy, with its resulting affirmation of the absolute good of material power and its accompanying commercialism and industrialism, mass production, and financial rule, is a merely mushroom growth upon the face of the earth, and the wide vistas opened by the telescope and the microscope both alike disclose at last nothing but blank walls enclosing a finite universe. Beyond is nothing—nothing discoverable by experiment, nothing measurable, nothing that the Materialist can know.

Nevertheless, Materialism is as much a philosophy and a religion as Christianity or Hinduism—a philosophy without metaphysic, a religion without the infinite (for the mathematician infinity is a mathematical trick). But it is a religion, and the productions of post-Reformation Europe are as much religious in their nature as the works of the Middle Ages or those of Asia.

Insistence on this fact is necessary if we are to understand the works of either East or West, of the present or of the past. And, strange as it may appear, Christians are the best equipped to gain such understanding, for by the very nature of their religion and philosophy they are able to apprehend both extremes. Unlike the Western Materialists, "the Church proceeds confidently in her doctrine of God." Unlike the Eastern Idealist, Christians hold that "matter and spirit are both real and both good." The Christian can understand and approve the enthusiasm of the Materialist for material good and goods and that of the mystic for spiritual reality and the immersion of the individual soul in the being of God.

The supremacy of matter over spirit or of spirit over matter is for the Materialist or the Idealist only achieved by the denial of the reality of one or the other. For the Christian, no less religious and no less philosophic than either, the dominance of the spiritual over the material, of mind over matter, is an article of faith, but matter is not therefore either evil or an illusion. Neither the errors of the Manichæans and the Puritans nor the speculations of Bishop Berkeley hold him. The whole history of the Christian Church is evidence of her struggles against these greatest temptations of thinking man—the temptation to the belief that the material life is all or to the belief that it is nothing. She emerges from the struggle the arbiter of East and West because she refuses the denials of either.

And the history of Christian art shows very clearly the Church's triumphant combination of the extremes. Buildings, such as the church of the Holy Wisdom at Constantinople, and the whole circle of mediæval cathedrals and abbey churches, are as notable for the daring with which they make play of material exigencies as they are notable on account of their spiritual sensibility. The cathedral church of Chartres or the parish church of St. Pierre in the same city may be viewed by the engineer or the sculptor with equal delight. It is true that the temples of India and the steel bridges of Europe and America are great architectural monuments. Nevertheless, the constructional daring of men of action is as conspicuously absent in the former as it is exclusively paramount in the latter—Christianity gave scope to both enthusiasms.

We are not here concerned to put forward Christian religion or the philosophy of St. Thomas Aquinas as the way, the truth, or the life. Our business here is to show that some philosophy, some religion is behind all human works, and is their primary instigation. Without some philosophy, some religion, nothing is done, nothing made, because nobody knows what to do or what to make, nobody knows what is good or what is bad; and if it be true that the Church exists in order that words may have a meaning, it may also be true that without philosophy and religion there is no meaning in human action.

Now it is held by many, especially of course by sceptical minds, that whether or no this or that philosophy or religion is or has been the ruling and effective motive in the making of human works, nevertheless such philosophy and religion are of no importance in relation to the works themselves: that the goodness or the badness of the works has nothing to do with either the religion or the philosophy prevalent among the workers. It is held that there is an æsthetic sense which is independent of good or bad, true or false. "A profound sense of form" is said to account for the goodness of the works of mediæval builders and sculptors, and the paintings of Ajanta and the glass of Chartres owe nothing to the ideas prevailing with their makers except their negligible and unintelligible subject-matter. "A profound sense of form!" And what is profound, what sensible, what formal? The phrase itself is meaningless without religion, without philosophy to gauge height and depth, sense and nonsense, the seen and the unseen. To such critics the subject is nothing; but to the workman, the artist, the subject has always been all in all. Unless he know what he is making he cannot make anything. Whether it be a church or only a tooth-pick he must know what it *is*; he must have it in his mind before he can begin, before he can even choose his material or lay his hand on a tool. And what a thing is, what things *are*, and, inevitably, whether they are good or bad, worth making or not, these questions bring him without fail to the necessity of making philosophical and religious decisions. We may accept the conclusions of others; it may, indeed, be better that we should do so—provided "we know in whom we believe"—but conclusions must be accepted or the workman can make no beginning. So far from it being true that religion and philosophy have no concern for the artist or he for them, it is only when a religion and philosophy have become the unifying principle of a nation that any great works, whether steel bridges or stone shrines, are possible, and the decay of human art follows immediately upon the weakening of men's grasp upon the motives of action.

The great art-works of twentieth-century Europe are the product of the great system of post-Reformation, post-Renaissance thought which is the religion and philosophy of materialism. Without that thought and its enthusiastic acceptance by widespread populations there could be none of those monuments of engineering and science which, while we may deplore the servile labour of the millions of workmen employed in their making, we unite to admire because they are admirable exhibitions of power. Similarly the pyramids of Eygpt could not have existed but for the theocracy of the ancient Egyptians and, while we profess to loathe their system of slave-labour, we rightly admire the pyramids because they are in themselves admirable monuments. So it is with the sculptures of India and Easter Island. So it is with the liturgical music of the Roman Church and the building achievements of the European middle age. So indeed it is with wireless telegraphy and the telephone; and all these things are the product of human activity directed, inspired, controlled, and only made possible by the religion and philosophy of their makers. And, as I have said, a most tremendous example will be the works of post-revolution Russia. It remains to be seen in what ways that product will differ from previous human achievements, but one thing is certain: it will be the direct expression of the religious affirmations and of the philosophy which are the determining principle, the soul of the Russian Revolution.

Now there are many who say that they like the sculptures of Sanchi but know nothing of Indian philosophy—that they like the windows of Chartres but loathe the Christian religion. They say that they know a good Chinese ivory when they see one, but care nothing for the ideas of Chinamen. They say that they like Westminster Abbey better than the Albert Memorial, but that they are very sure that the ideas of Prince Albert were in every way more enlightened than those of Edward the Third. Therefore they hold it to be clear that philosophical ideas or religious beliefs have little to do with works. Thus they come to the conclusion that "a profound sense of form" is all that is required, and that the thing called "form" is independent of intellectual or religious belief. This conclusion, however, seems to help very little; for if a thing has a certain form (and a material thing must have some form) the form must be the right form or the wrong, a good form or a bad, and when we say that a certain thing has right or good form we can only mean that it has the form proper to it if it really is what it purports to be. A profound sense of form means therefore a profound sense of what is right form, and that means a profound sense of what form a certain thing, being what it is, ought to have. But to know what form a thing ought to have involves the knowledge of what the thing that is to be made really *is*, and that involves knowledge of its significance and purpose, the place where it is to go and the material of which it is to be made. But knowledge of the significance and purpose of things is, for man, a rational and not merely animal being, conditioned by general as well as particular considerations, and it is precisely a profound sense of these general considerations, as well as of the particular considerations, which is necessary to the production of any good and right work.

If we deny that the forms of things owe anything of their quality of beauty, that is their power to please him who sees them (for the beautiful thing is that which being seen pleases, *id quod visum placet*), to the possession by their makers of some knowledge of what they were making and some good will in the execution; if we deny, that is to say, that good sense and good will have any part in the production of beautiful works; if we say that a thing can have good form and yet this good form, at least as regards its *goodness*, have nothing to do with what the thing is, then we are, in effect and in fact, denying that the thing we call beauty has anything to do with the mind, and therefore that beauty is simply a kind of visible or audible sugar, if we like things sweet, or a kind of visible or audible salt if we prefer them savoury. In such a view a beautiful man is not "a man as he ought to be" (i.e. a man deprived of nothing that he ought to have—ugliness being simply privation), but is, as a thing of beauty, not a man at all, but simply a contraption of shapes and colours causing a charming physical excitement in the same way as does the light reflected in spilt petroleum.

This is no mean excitement, and I am not decrying it. Many physical sensations are highly delightful and only bad people regret it. But that this is *all* we mean or that this is what we *chiefly* mean by the word beauty is not to be believed. Let it be granted, and granted without any demur whatever, let it be granted with the utmost enthusiasm, that there is this physical kind of beautifulness. That is very good; but is that all?

If it be all, then two things follow. First, we must deny the name of beauty to aeroplanes and all such things (bicycles, spoon-baits, locomotives, spider-webs, beehives, flying-buttresses and the stone vaults they prop up, flowers and animals, and the bodies of men and women) whose only claim to be called beautiful is on account of the fine and impressive and immediately obvious perfection of their functional adaptation. For this perfection being obvious to the mind alone (it is certainly not sensually obvious), and yet beauty, according to our supposition having nothing to do with the mind, it necessarily follows that those things, however obviously perfect, cannot be called beautiful. Second, we must admit that good taste in pictures is precisely and exactly the same in kind as a healthy animal taste in food.

But these conclusions are obviously absurd. Bones and spider-webs and animals and man-made machinery are in fact beautiful—that is, pleasing when seen, and however grand and venerable a thing it is to know a good wine or cheese from a

XIII bad one, it remains true that it requires an intelligent person to have pleasure in pictures or buildings, but a mere animal has pleasure in food.

Nevertheless, if we say that beauty is dependent upon good sense and good will in the workman we do not in the least mean that the production or experience of beauty depends upon ratiocination by the workman or that its perception depends upon ratiocination by the beholder. The thing called beauty is not the term of a process of logical or discursive reasoning. The beautiful thing is reasonable; it is the product of a rational soul, but it is not therefore reasoned.

On the other hand, we do not mean that the beautiful is perceived or experienced, either by the workman or his customer, by a power of intuition such as is not properly within human competence at all, but is the prerogative of the angels. The perception of the beautiful is neither by means of ratiocination nor of angelic intuition.[1]

[1] A man who has knowledge of the beautiful is commonly said to have "good taste." It is significant that among the Hindus the word *Rasa*, which primarily means taste or savour, also means beauty. The connection appears to be the following: the real being or essence of things is held to be not in their material, ponderable or measurable appearance, but in an immaterial or spiritual quality. Among things known to men their taste or savour seems to be of an immaterial or quasi-spiritual nature compared with their bulk,

The perception of what is prudent is by means of a kind of *common sense*. But by common sense we do not mean a thing of no importance, because "commonplace," vulgar, or lacking in subtlety, but a sense depending upon judgments and interpretations so multifarious and of such infinite complexity that it achieves a quality of almost infallible rectitude, and as we say *vox populi, vox Dei* and *securus judicat orbis terrarum*, so we hold common sense to be generally more certain in its judgments than any individual effort of ratiocination. XIII

Now the knowledge of the beautiful is of this nature, and as it is by what we call common sense that men appreciate what is in accordance with right conduct, that is to say with Prudence, that is to say with "man's last end," that is to say with man's destiny as child of God and inheritor of the Kingdom of Heaven, so it is by a *common sensibility*, as I may now call it, that men appreciate what is in accord-

their weight or their measurable shape. Hence the taste of an apple or the scent of a rose was among simple people thought to be its essence (in Europe also perfumes are sometimes called essences). In the same way the quality which among visible or audible things seems to be more their essence, their real being, than their measure or their weight or their physical properties, is called their taste or savour (*Rasa*), that is to say, their Beauty, and as one tastes or savours the essence of an apple so one savours the beauty (i.e. essence) of a sculpture.

ance with right making, that is to say with art, that is to say with the nature of things as manifesting the creative love of God, that is to say Beauty itself. For though our natural modesty makes us shy of such high phrases, it is without doubt that as all goodness in men is a reflection of the goodness of God and an earnest of man's godward direction, so all beauty is a reflection of the divine beauty, and (apart from his animal pleasure, which is simply that of a creature in whom is implanted a will to live and therefore a satisfaction in those things which foster his life and a dislike of those which are inimical to it) man's pleasure in things seen or heard is in fact only understandable when explained as a pleasure in what is in accordance with reality, pure Being, God Himself.

And as we fail in good will by reason of every kind of self will, and as we fail in good sense by reason of both ill will and the necessary limitations of a finite nature, so we fail in common sense and in common sensibility. The sense of Prudence, that is, the sense of right doing, what we call common sense, is really no more common than the sense of Art, that is, the sense of right making.[1]

In response to police supervision we have developed a high sense of what is in accordance with

[1] See Appendix.

public safety—moral safety no less than physical safety. In response to the exigencies of commerce we have developed a high sense of what is in accordance with structural economy (what else is the science of engineering?). In both these spheres we may be said to have excellent *taste*—a taste which would have astonished our ancestors and will doubtless astonish posterity. The locomotive called "*the Rocket*" and the first motor-cars or automobiles are to us not only comic; they are also exceedingly pathetic in their primitive and barbarous lack of structural economy and, were it not that man is always impressed by what is much bigger than himself, the vast, fat, round pillars of Norman churches would seem to us equally pathetic.

But in the face of such high developments of taste it is inevitable that development in other directions should be less notable. A great epoch of commercial enterprise, while it may develop a great system of roads, aqueducts, and mechanical contrivances, may also develop a great system of common law and public safety (in these respects twentieth-century England is not unlike third-century Rome), but it cannot expect also to witness the development of a high sensibility in handiworks. Such things are necessarily crushed to death between the mill-stones of mass production and mass marketing. And in such circumstances what are called the "fine" arts will suffer most of all; for whereas the primary purposes of chairs and tables can be defined by measurement and therefore useful chairs may be made by the million, the primary purpose of pictures and poems is in the nature of things unmeasurable and therefore, unless a high common-sensibility be developed in such regard, good poems and good pictures must be unobtainable or remain as they do to-day, the rare and eccentric product of the fastidious genius who by a peculiar and no longer *common* sense smells out the standards of a civilisation less wrapt up in weights and measures than his own.

But here again misunderstanding must be avoided. The line of division between arts and fine arts, between the fine arts and the servile arts, is not so clear in practice as it is in theory. In theory we may lay it down, glibly enough, that the servile arts are those which serve the body and the fine arts those which serve the mind. We may argue therefore that anything which has any kind of physical utility is the product of a servile art, and that those things which we make solely for delight, elevation, instruction, or amusement are works of fine art. But in practice—in practice the two spheres are hardly separable. There is an element of delightfulness deliberately contrived by the workman in nearly all the things men make to serve their bodily needs, and there is an element of physical serviceableness in many works which seem to owe their existence to the needs of the mind alone. Consider for example the art of architecture. What art could be more obviously servile than that which keeps the rain out of our houses, or more free and therefore "fine" than that which contrived the high-pointed roof which keeps the rain off the tower of Salisbury? Nevertheless, the categories are distinct and common sense confirms the distinction. And, however mixed may be the motives which inspire and provoke the majority of man's works, it remains true that a drainage system and a musical symphony belong to different orders of things.

The distinction between servile art and fine art runs parallel with that between sense and sensibility, between ratiocination and rationality. The distinction, after all, is primarily between matter and spirit, and it is precisely because man is compounded of both matter and spirit that he is confronted by this dilemma. A good chair would seem to be simply a matter of measurement—the seat of the

XIII chair should fit the seat of the man. What more is there than that? (What more, indeed, can a leader of commerce know unless he employ priests and politicians and a whole gang of humane persons to tell him—or unless he "boil down" the whole gang into the person of one tame "art adviser"?) But a man is not simply a corpse—he may be a father or even a bishop, and what he needs is something suitable rather than something which merely fits. At once the mind is involved in judgments of a spiritual order; it is no longer absorbed simply in measurement. In the end the chair may seem more delightful than useful. Nevertheless, the good chair-maker must never desert or despise his function of physical service; for such serviceableness is the quality without which his work is nothing—*sine qua non.*

On the other hand, a good poem would seem to be simply a matter of mind—the meaning of the poem should suit the mind of the man. But the mind of man touches the Infinite Mind and meanings are infinite in number. If the chair-maker has a spiritual soul, so the poet has a physical body. The one is dragged heavenwards; the other is tied to the earth. Words are no less material than the stuff of which chairs are made. Here again is a *sine qua non.* The chief difference between chair-maker and poet is this: that the poet is primarily concerned with spiritual judgments—words, letters, ink, and paper are simply vehicles for his utterance; he is dependent upon them because otherwise his meaning is incommunicable. He may love the vehicle and make it the means to more meaning, but essentially the poem is purely compounded of the stuff of the mind.

On the other hand, the chair-maker is primarily concerned with material judgments; but being a man he is inevitably dragged upwards and forced to utter spiritual judgments. This is the beautiful—that which being seen pleases. And it is *man* who sees and is pleased—man to whom eternally, and therefore here and now, nothing can be pleasing but what his mind approves. Poetry and chair-making—these are as it were the two poles. Between these two are all other arts; and all arts are compounded of the essences of poetry and chair-making.

The enlightenment of the leading men of our time is with regard to the things of interest to a shop-keeping civilisation whose philosophy is Materialism. The religion of commercial England finds its profoundest expression in its great works of engineering and applied science. Such a monument as the memorial to Prince Albert in Hyde Park is

XIII simply a mistake—a thing the nineteenth century was foolish to attempt. The Royal Albert Bridge at Saltash is that prince's proper memorial.

On the other hand, the enlightenment of the thirteenth century in Europe or of the fifth century before Christ in India was with regard to the things of interest to men among whom commerce was little developed and even less venerated. We have princes of commerce: they had princes of States. We have soap and marmalade kings: they had kings of men. They believed in an eternal life for which this life is a preparation. We believe that this life is all. The religion and philosophy of mediæval Europe or of India finds its profoundest expression therefore in works quite different from ours. We do wrong to compare the Albert Memorial with Westminster Abbey, or the Houses of Parliament with the tope of Sanchi. We do wrong because we do ourselves an injustice. Imitation Gothic architecture is a monument to our sentimental regard for our ancient past and does not represent the religion and philosophy which inspire our civilisation. But, for example, the bridge across the river St. Lawrence at Quebec (an improved version of the bridge across the Firth of Forth) would stand comparison with any western cathedral or eastern temple. And in making such a comparison the important, the fundamental part borne by religion and philosophy in the conception and execution of human works becomes evident. Could such a thing as the bridge at Quebec have been built in any other time than ours or under the inspiration and direction of any other enthusiasms? Could the church at Chartres have come out of any other womb than that of the Christian religion?

But is not Christianity still with us to-day and were there not money-lenders in the eleventh century? Yes, but Christianity is as powerless to-day as money-lenders were despised then. Christianity is powerless now because it commands nothing but its altars. Financiers were powerless then because they commanded nothing but their gold and went about in fear of their skins. These things were all changed because religion and philosophy were changed.

It is useless here going into the question of the corruption of the mediæval Church, and the consequent almost complete loss of Europe to Christianity. The disorder in the century following the physical disaster of the "Black Death" and the spiritual disaster of the "Great Schism" may alone be considered sufficient cause for the destruction of the mediæval unity, and there were many other causes equally considerable. Men of commerce and money-lenders were men of political power long before the Plague. The temporal power of princes was rivalled by that of ecclesiastics long before Avignon.

Among the early Christians the desire for money was held to be the root of all evil; to-day that desire is instilled into every schoolboy. This may be right or wrong, but it cannot be called the same. And as the Christian religion and philosophy lost their hold on men's minds, so the works done under their inspiration became decadent—fanciful, vulgar, pretty, elegant, extravagant, grandiose—until a new religion and a new philosophy enthralled us, and a new enthusiasm inspired new and better works.

The mediæval inspiration had obviously long been lost when such a jew-jaw as Henry VII's Chapel at Westminster could popularly be supposed a suitable house for the relics of a saint. The classicalism of Inigo Jones at old St. Paul's was at least a return to something more venerable, because more austere, less frivolous, than the commercialised Gothic of the fourteenth and fifteenth centuries.

And when the commercial idea finally won its victory and threw away the shackles of both Church and King, then all was ready for the onrush of mechanical invention and the seizure of those stores of capital we call coal and oil. A new art and a new architecture were made as possible as they were inevitable.

These things being so, the whole business of modern "art" education is seen to be foolishness. Painting and sculpture, music and letters, are in our time necessarily merely idiosyncratic. Such works are necessarily merely "self-expression," that is to say, the expression of isolated and eccentric minds. The proper expression of our age is in its communal works of mechanical skill. These are our works of art. The factory is our art school. Painting and sculptures are for us mere fal-lals, curiosities suitable for museums. There is no public place for them. They mean nothing to anybody but to their makers and a coterie of æsthetes.

Yet, strange as it may seem, painters and sculptors were not very great dukes even in mediæval Europe or India. Their great works were the product of popular poetic infection. There was no such thing as a school specially devoted to the learning of a thing called Art. Buildings and workshops were their art-schools and the ideas to be expressed, made manifest in material, were not specially those of the workmen, the artists, but, as to-day in the case of science and mechanics, of whole populations. Individual prowess was doubtless applauded, but it was seen in right perspective—a thing of small importance compared with the right-thinking of the community. A mediæval cathedral, like the bridge at Quebec or even the common domestic sewing-machine, expresses the genius of a whole people.

And if our steel engineering may stand comparison with mediæval stone building, inasmuch as both are authentic expressions of the peoples who made them and show the differences of religion and philosophy in our age as compared with another, so may the sculptures and paintings of mediæval Europe be compared with those of the Hindus and Buddhists. But in this case what is chiefly notable are similarities not differences. Mediæval Hindu and European images are the same in *kind*. Both are made according to hieratic canon, both are devoid of idiosyncrasy. Both are negligent of anatomical verisimilitude. Both are of public rather than private significance. Both are concerned with the expression of conceptions of general importance and widespread belief, and not with personal and particular likings. "Life-like" portraiture is rare (the Great Seal of Henry IV is identical with that of Henry V except for the change of numerals—they are symbols of Kingship rather than of *a* King—and the countless images of the Buddha are like no individual). Both are entirely inæsthetic, in the sense that in neither case were the artists consciously concerned to produce things of beauty for beauty's sake. Beauty in both cases is the radiance of things made as they ought to be made. The best works and the best periods are those in which the nature of the thing to be made is best *known* and most poignantly *expressed*—"the time and the place and the loved one all together."

Why is the Tower Bridge in London obviously ugly but because it is obviously foolish? Its makers had more respect for the adjacent mediæval castle than for their own handiwork. Thus there are many bad works in all periods of human history, and in all cases their ugliness is a privation—they are lacking in what they ought to have. Bad works are the product of men who *do not know what they are making* or who *do not care*. An early Christian crucifix is a better work of art simply because it is a better crucifix. *Look after goodness and truth, and beauty will take care of herself.*

APPENDIX

UNUS EST ARTIFEX DEUS

HOWEVER *valuable religion and philosophy may be as ruling powers in civilisation and as disciplines for workmen, how can they be the cause of that quality in human works which is called Beauty?*

I. The human soul (or mind) is a union of intellect and will. The intellect is a faculty having *truth* for its object. The will is a faculty having *good* for its object. Of what faculty is *Beauty* the object?

Beauty is a union of the true and the good, and the faculty which has beauty for its object is the whole and undivided mind. For as the true and the good are united in beauty, so intellect and will must necessarily be united for beauty's discernment and apprehension.

The apprehension of beauty is in function of man's soul as such. Beauty is neither purely intelligible nor purely desirable. It is both known and loved.

Therefore the appreciation of the beautiful is connatural to man, and his idea of *bliss* (Heaven, Nirvana, Paradise) is beauty unalloyed. The ecstasy of sexual union is a type of it and the idea of music is inseparable from our idea of heaven.

We need not here discuss the question of the possibility of false notions of the beautiful. Because men make mistakes, truth is not therefore non-existent. Because men commit sin, it does not follow that there is no good. And because men differ in their opinions as to what is beautiful, we need not conclude that beauty is no more than a physical satisfaction like the sweetness of sugar. APP.

II. These things being understood, we must next consider what is the real nature of man's creative activity. As well as by its gratuitousness man's art (that is to say, the things man *makes* as distinct from the things he *does*, and especially those things which he makes as ends in themselves as distinct from those things which he makes as tools and contrivances to do things with—though even these things may be thought of as worth making for their own sakes and not merely as means to ends) man's art resembles that of God by its originality. Even though it be true that man derives all his ideas from things known to him by means of his senses whereas the ideas of God actually create things, nevertheless, what man makes is the product of his mind and is not merely a reflection of what he has seen with his eyes or heard with his ears. The idea of the artist is, as the philosopher says, "an idea *formative* of things and not *formed* by them,"[1] and the work of art is, as I have said elsewhere,[2] a product of the imagination and not of the photographer's camera.

We have then two things: the mind and the works of the mind—the mind of God and things derived directly from His ideas; the mind of man and things derived directly from man's ideas (though man's ideas are derived from the things which God has made.

III. In the previous essay we have treated of art as it exists in human society, the product of men working for their living, making things for the necessities and amenities of human existence in this world. The thesis of that essay is that, under the conditions of human life, without philosophy and religion men will not only not make things well, but will not make them at all. Philosophy gives man a sense of his relation to the universe; religion gives him a sense of his relation to God. Philosophy would lead man to wisdom; religion would give him the experience of divinity. Without philosophy man cannot know *what* he makes, without religion he cannot know *why*. It remains to show in what way philosophy and religion are the instigation of man's

[1] Maritain, *Art and Scholasticism*, Eng. trans., p. 89.

[2] "Sculpture and the Living Model," p. 97.

works regarded, not as useful objects, or even objects whose purpose is to elevate, instruct, or amuse, but as objects of beauty existing for themselves alone. How may philosophy and religion be called the instigation of beauty in human works?

The statement of philosophy is not to be confused with philosophy itself, and the formularies and practices of religious sects are not to be confused with the experience of God. Statements, formularies, practices may be works of beauty; they are not beauty's instigation. But of course it is immediately clear that the instigation of beauty, as of the true and the good, is God Himself. God is beauty, as He is love and strength and wisdom and honour, and "the divine beauty is the cause of all being."

To say, therefore, that philosophy and religion are the effective motive in human works, works of love no less than works of power, of beauty no less than of usefulness, is simply to say that God is the instigator of all good works, and that the good workman is the man of God, and this is, in an especial manner, true in respect of those works whereof beauty is the formal cause. "After God all paternity in heaven and earth is named," and this does most precisely mean that all creative acts have God for their author. The human act of begetting is a type of divine creative power. The act of the artist in the creative imagination is, as the schoolmen pointed out, the nearest human counterpart. And, though it be true that his imagination is nourished and sustained by vision and hearing and all the senses, because and in so far as the idea of the artist is not formed by what he sees but is formative of what he makes, so and so far is he actually a creator—the father indeed of his works. But it is only in respect of beauty that man is a creator. The search for truth is not invention; it is the search for what *is*. All good deeds are but means to ends; they are not ends in themselves. Only the beautiful is an end in itself and only beauty is ever new. That which is beautiful pleases when seen, and it is the mind which sees and is pleased. The mind, compounded of intellect and will, sees and is pleased by the beautiful—the beautiful compounded of the true and the good. But there is no need for the good workman to talk about it or even to be able to do so, and as the good man prays without knowing that he is praying, so the good workman may work well without knowing that he is wise or remembering that God exists.

Nevertheless, for the very reason that "some God must be the guide," that God is indeed the only artificer, and that all that is not good is simply ungodly, it is necessary for men to defend themselves against what may hinder or destroy contemplation, and to that end, for that defence, statements and formularies, creeds and all pious exercises have been invented. Since Adam sinned few have been privileged to walk with God in the garden. For the most part men have been obliged to find God in the work demanded of them by their fellows. Therefore we may say this: that philosophy and religion are the effective motive in human works in two ways. First, as providing a statement and discipline in accordance with which ordinary workmen may be moved to serve God and thus become the instruments of His creative power, and second, as being the orientation of the mind towards God and the living experience of Him so that the workman, or artist, collaborates with God in creating.

The Trobriander who carves spoons and spears is undoubtedly inspired, instigated, motived, and made effective by the philosophy and religion which, however disturbed by economic circumstance, is indeed the very soul of his culture. Such islanders are, as much as the sculptors of Elura or Chartres, though less well informed and less conscious of themselves, activated by divine wisdom and the experience of divinity. In statement their

APP. philosophy is infantile; in practice their religion is barbarous; but as workmen they walk with God.

So also, at the other extreme, in places where men are divorced altogether from traditional culture, where traditions are decayed, civilisation corrupted by commercialism and industrialism, and individual artists a prey to vice and unbelief, where self-consciousness in the artist is carried to its highest possible limit and, owing to the degradation of all other workmen to subhuman conditions of intellectual irresponsibility, self-consciousness, and therefore self-expression, is thought to be the very core of art work—in such places, among such men, such artists, philosophy and religion, though no longer the philosophy and religion of a tribe or of a nation, are the instigation, the effective motive of the work. No more than with the Trobriander or the mediæval European is there necessarily any statement of principles "at the tip of the tongue"; nor is it necessary that, like the pious Hindu craftsman, the artist should practise a stated discipline of religious meditation and dedication before he begins a work (though there is little doubt that it would be good for the work if he could do so). But as workman, as artist, his very self-consciousness determines him towards God, is an identification of himself as creator with the Creator of all things. Philosophy and religion are the instigation of his work; for he is himself philosopher, he is himself man of God. His work is wisdom itself, is God made manifest.

What of the charlatan in this line of business? The artist who pretends a mysticism which is unreal is not merely deceiving his fellow men; he is, presumably for the sake of money, making Charity a thing of mud.

What of the Philistine? Physical comfort and grandeur are, for him, the measure of all things. For him *all* artists are charlatans, and the only bread he will give them is stones. Cézanne, like St. Stephen, was thus fed.

And what of the cowards and the fatigued? They are afraid to face Love; they are too tired to rebuild His house. They do not so much as know if there be a Holy Ghost. They fall back upon an "economic interpretation of history," and are satisfied to live by bread alone.

www.ingramcontent.com/pod-product-compliance
Lightning Source LLC
LaVergne TN
LVHW091118080826
845145LV00008B/1964

9781887593441